HOTEL HOUSEKEEPING FOR FUTURE MANAGERS

PANKAJ BEHL

BLUEROSE PUBLISHERS
India | U.K.

Copyright © Pankaj Behl 2023

All rights reserved by author. No part of this publication may be reproduced, stored in a retrieval system or transmitted in any form or by any means, electronic, mechanical, photocopying, recording or otherwise, without the prior permission of the author. Although every precaution has been taken to verify the accuracy of the information contained herein, the publisher assume no responsibility for any errors or omissions. No liability is assumed for damages that may result from the use of information contained within.

BlueRose Publishers takes no responsibility for any damages, losses, or liabilities that may arise from the use or misuse of the information, products, or services provided in this publication.

For permissions requests or inquiries regarding this publication,
please contact:

BLUEROSE PUBLISHERS
www.BlueRoseONE.com
info@bluerosepublishers.com
+91 8882 898 898
+4407342408967

ISBN: 978-93-5989-900-8

Cover design: Tahira
Typesetting: Tanya Raj Upadhyay

First Edition: October 2023

Hotel Housekeeping- For Future Managers

Purpose & Scope

The purpose of this book is to serve as a comprehensive guide for students & housekeeping professionals to maintain cleanliness & orderliness in hotel rooms, common areas & facilities. The book contains detailed instructions & procedures on how to perform various cleaning tasks, including but not limited to dusting, vacuuming, changing bed linens, cleaning bathrooms, & restocking amenities.

In addition, the book includes guidelines on proper handling of cleaning equipment, chemicals & supplies to ensure safety & prevent damage to hotel property. It also provides information on how to report maintenance issues or damages found during cleaning & how to communicate effectively with guests & other staff members.

Furthermore, the hotel housekeeping book emphasizes the importance of maintaining high standards of cleanliness & hygiene in order to provide guests with a comfortable & enjoyable stay. It outlines the key principles of customer service & professionalism that housekeeping staff should adhere to when interacting with guests.

Overall, the purpose of this hotel housekeeping book is to provide a clear & concise reference guide for housekeeping professionals to perform their duties efficiently & effectively, while maintaining the highest standards of cleanliness, safety & customer service.

About the Author

Pankaj Behl is a dedicated and experienced hotel housekeeper with a keen eye for detail and a passion for ensuring guests have a comfortable and memorable stay. With over 13 years of experience in the hospitality industry, Pankaj has worked in various renowned brands like Leela, Marriott, Taj, IHG & Hyatt honing his skills and perfecting his craft.

Having started his career as a housekeeping trainee, Pankaj quickly rose through the ranks due to his exceptional work ethic and commitment to excellence. He understands the importance of creating a clean and inviting environment for guests, and his attention to detail is unmatched.

Throughout his career, Pankaj has witnessed the inner workings of the hotel industry, gaining invaluable insights into the behind-the-scenes operations that contribute to a seamless guest experience. His vast knowledge of housekeeping procedures, room cleanliness standards, and effective organization methods has made him a trusted resource among his peers.

Pankaj is known for his exceptional customer service skills and his ability to anticipate guests' needs. He believes that a clean and well-maintained room is not just a place to sleep but a sanctuary where guests can relax and feel at home. His dedication to providing a top-notch guest experience has earned him recognition and appreciation from both colleagues and hotel guests.

Outside of his profession, Pankaj enjoys exploring new destinations and experiencing different cultures. His travels have provided him with a broader perspective on the importance of hospitality and the role of housekeeping in creating a welcoming environment for guests from all walks of life.

Pankaj is excited to share his knowledge and expertise with fellow hotel housekeepers and aspiring professionals in the industry. Through this book, he aims to provide practical tips, effective cleaning techniques, and insights into maintaining high standards of cleanliness in hotels.

Connect with Pankaj Behl on LinkedIn (linkedin.com/in/pankaj-behl-10047bb3) to stay updated on his latest projects and to join a community of passionate hotel professionals. He welcomes your feedback, questions, and stories from the industry.

TOPICS

1. **Introduction to Hotel Housekeeping** - This chapter introduces the concept of hotel housekeeping & explains the importance of cleanliness & organization in a hotel setting.

2. **Housekeeping Management** - This chapter can provide an overview of housekeeping management, including staffing, training and scheduling.

3. **Cleaning Techniques & Equipment** - This chapter covers different cleaning techniques & tools used in hotel housekeeping, such as vacuum cleaners, mops & cleaning chemicals.

4. **Room Cleaning Procedures** - This chapter provides step-by-step instructions for cleaning hotel rooms, including changing linens, dusting,& cleaning bathrooms.

5. **Laundry Services** - This chapter covers the process of washing, drying, & folding hotel linens & towels, as well as handling guest laundry requests.

6. **Linen & Uniform Room** – This chapters explains the functioning of Linen & Uniform room, process of issuing uniforms, selection of uniforms, types of uniforms, layout of uniform room, recycling discarded linen types of stains & their treatments.

7. **Inventory Management** - This chapter explains how housekeeping staff should manage supplies & equipment, such as cleaning products, towels & bedding.

8. **Safety & Security** - This chapter covers safety protocols for housekeeping staff, such as proper use of cleaning chemicals & safe lifting techniques, as well as security procedures for guest rooms & common areas.

9. **Communication & Customer Service** - This chapter provides guidance on how housekeeping staff can communicate effectively with guests & colleagues, as well as tips for providing excellent customer service.

10. **Environment Sustainability** -This chapter covers how housekeeping staff can reduce the hotel's environmental impact by using eco-friendly cleaning products and implementing energy-saving practices.

11. **Brand standards** - This chapter covers the various elements that are critical in defining the brand standards of any hotel.

12. **Housekeeping pantry & trolley management** – This chapter explains how the pantries & trollies are set as per standards & how does it contributes towards the overall operations

13. **Preventive maintenance program** – This chapter explains a proactive approach that involves scheduled inspections, maintenance, and repairs to prevent equipment failures and minimize downtime, extending the lifespan of assets and reducing the likelihood of costly breakdowns.

14. **Pest Controlling** –This chapter explains the use of preventive measures, treatments, and extermination techniques, ensuring a hygienic and pest-free environment.

15. **Façade Cleaning** –This chapter explains the process of removing dirt, grime, and other debris from the exterior surfaces of buildings, including windows, walls, and architectural features, using specialized cleaning techniques and equipment, to maintain a clean and visually appealing appearance while ensuring the structural integrity of the building.

16. **Marble Polishing** –This chapter explains the restoration and enhancement of the natural shine and smoothness of marble surfaces through the use of abrasive compounds, polishing pads, and techniques to remove scratches, stains, and imperfections.

17. **Carpet Shampooing** – This chapter explains the deep cleaning method used for carpets to make it look clean, fresh, and revitalized.

18. **Flower Arrangement** – This chapter explains the art of creatively arranging cut flowers and foliage in various styles, designs, and containers to create visually appealing and harmonious compositions.

19. **Landscaping** – This chapter explains a very important component of hotel housekeeping that focuses on maintaining and enhancing the outdoor areas of the hotel property.

20. **Chandelier cleaning** - Chapter chandelier cleaning involves the meticulous process of removing dust, dirt, and grime from intricate lighting fixtures, restoring their sparkle and enhancing their aesthetic appeal, creating a captivating ambiance in the space they adorn.

21. **Snagging** - This chapter snagging explains how to identify and rectify any defects or issues before the project is handed over to the client, ensuring the highest quality and compliance with standards.

22. **Lost & found management** – This chapter explains the systematic handling and organization of misplaced or forgotten items by guests, ensuring proper documentation, storage, and attempts to reunite them with their owners, providing a reliable and efficient service to enhance guest satisfaction and maintain the hotel's reputation.

23. **Standard operating procedure** – This chapter explains how to define prescribed methods, guidelines, and best practices to ensure consistency, efficiency, and quality in performing a specific task or process within an organization.

24. **DND Procedure** – This chapter explains the procedure followed in hotels & involves respecting guests' privacy by refraining from entering their rooms when the DND sign is displayed.

25. **Lobby scenting** – This chapter explains the intentional use of fragrances or scents in the hotel lobby to create a pleasant and welcoming atmosphere, enhancing the overall guest experience and leaving a lasting impression through the sense of smell.

26. **Latest trends & technologies** – This chapter explains the latest trends and technologies in hotel housekeeping include the use of robotic cleaners and automated systems for efficient and time-saving room cleaning processes

27. **Audits** - This chapter explains systematic inspections and evaluations of cleaning standards, procedures, and overall cleanliness to ensure compliance with industry standards and maintain a high level of hygiene and guest satisfaction.

Table of Contents

1. Introduction to Hotel Housekeeping 1
2. Housekeeping Management 7
3. Cleaning Techniques & Equipments 20
4. Room Cleaning Procedures 25
5. Laundry Services 34
6. Linen & Uniform Room 40
7. Inventory Management 49
8. Safety & Security 52
9. Communication & Customer Service 59
10. Environment Sustainability 64
11. Brand Standards 68
12. Housekeeping Pantry & Trolley Management 70
13. Preventive Maintenance Program 72
14. Pest Controlling 77
15. Façade Cleaning 84
16. Marble Polishing 86
17. Carpet Shampooing 88
18. Flower Arrangement 90
19. Landscaping 95
20. Chandelier Cleaning 99
21. Snagging 101
22. Lost & Found Management 103
23. Standard Operating Procedures 105
24. Do Not Disturb Procedure 110
25. Lobby Scenting 112
26. Latest Trends & Technologies 114
27. Audits 116

CHAPTER 1
Introduction to Hotel Housekeeping

Hotel housekeeping is a critical function in the hospitality industry that involves the cleaning, maintenance, and organization of guest rooms and common areas. The primary goal of hotel housekeeping is to ensure that guests are provided with a clean, comfortable, and safe environment during their stay.

Effective hotel housekeeping requires a dedicated and well-trained team of staff who are skilled in using the latest cleaning techniques and equipment. Housekeeping staff must be detail-oriented and able to work efficiently and quickly to meet the demands of a busy hotel.

In addition to keeping guest rooms and common areas clean, housekeeping staff must also be attentive to guest needs and requests, such as providing extra towels or pillows, or responding to maintenance issues in a timely manner.

Overall, hotel housekeeping plays a critical role in the guest experience, and a well-managed and efficient housekeeping department can help to ensure that guests have a pleasant and enjoyable stay at the hotel.

Cleanliness is of utmost importance in hotels, and it plays a vital role in ensuring guest satisfaction, health, and safety. The following are some of the reasons why cleanliness is essential in hotels:

1. **Guest satisfaction** - Cleanliness is one of the top factors that guests consider when choosing a hotel. A clean and well-maintained hotel room can help to create a positive impression on guests, and can contribute to their overall satisfaction with their stay.

2. **Health and safety** - Dirty or unsanitary conditions in hotels can pose health risks to guests, as well as staff. Cleanliness can help to reduce the risk of illnesses caused by bacteria, viruses, and other harmful microorganisms.

3. **Reputation** - A hotel's reputation can be affected by its cleanliness levels. Negative reviews or feedback from guests about cleanliness can harm a hotel's reputation and can lead to a decline in business.

4. **Compliance with regulations** - Hotels are required to comply with health and safety regulations, and cleanliness is a crucial aspect of these regulations. Failure to meet these requirements can result in fines and legal action.

5. **Maintenance** - Cleanliness can also help to maintain the condition of hotel rooms and facilities, reducing the need for repairs and replacement of equipment and furnishings.

Overall, cleanliness is essential for hotels to create a welcoming and safe environment for guests and staff, maintain a positive reputation, comply with regulations, and preserve the condition of their facilities.

The Housekeeping Department

The housekeeping department is an essential part of a hotel's operation, and its main function is to ensure that hotel rooms and common areas are clean, well-maintained, and organized. The following is an overview of the housekeeping department and its functions:

1. **Room cleaning** - One of the primary functions of the housekeeping department is to clean and maintain guest rooms. This includes making beds, cleaning bathrooms, dusting, and vacuuming or sweeping floors.

2. **Laundry services** - Housekeeping staff also manages the hotel's laundry services, which involves washing, drying, folding, and ironing linens, towels, and other hotel items.

3. **Public area cleaning** - Housekeeping staff is responsible for maintaining the cleanliness and organization of public areas, such as lobbies, hallways, and dining areas.

4. **Inventory management** - The housekeeping department manages the inventory of cleaning supplies, linens, towels, and other items necessary for cleaning and maintaining the hotel's rooms and common areas.

5. **Maintenance** - The housekeeping department also reports maintenance issues to the maintenance staff or hotel management to ensure that repairs and maintenance are done promptly.

6. **Training and staffing** - The housekeeping department is responsible for training and managing housekeeping staff, including scheduling, monitoring performance, and ensuring that staff comply with hotel policies and standards.

7. **Pest Control** - Housekeeping staff is trained to identify and report signs of pest infestations. They take preventive measures and coordinate with the maintenance department or external pest control services to address any pest issues.

8. **Lost and Found** - Housekeeping staff handles lost and found items in guest rooms and public areas. They properly store and maintain lost items, and coordinate with the front desk to return them to guests or follow established protocols.

9. **Adherence to Standards** - Housekeeping departments follow established cleanliness and hygiene standards, including those set by hotel management, brand standards, and regulatory requirements. They perform regular inspections to ensure compliance.

10. **Landscaping** - It is an important component of hotel housekeeping that focuses on maintaining and enhancing the outdoor areas of the hotel property. It involves the design, installation, and maintenance of gardens, lawns, plants, trees, and other outdoor features.

11. **Flower Decoration** – Flower decoration in hotels requires the expertise of skilled florists who understand design principles, color palettes, and the proper care and handling of flowers. It adds a sense of luxury, elegance, and freshness to various areas of the hotel, enhancing the overall guest experience and creating lasting memories.

Overall, the housekeeping department plays a critical role in maintaining a clean, safe, and welcoming environment for guests and staff in a hotel. Effective management of the department is essential to ensure that the hotel's cleanliness standards are met, and guests are satisfied with their stay.

The hierarchy of a hotel housekeeping department typically follows a structure with various positions, each having specific responsibilities and reporting to higher-ranking positions. The hierarchy may vary depending on the size and complexity of the hotel. Here is a common hierarchy of a hotel housekeeping department:

1. **Executive Housekeeper / Director of Housekeeping:**

   - At the top of the hierarchy is the Executive Housekeeper or Director of Housekeeping. This position oversees the entire housekeeping department and is responsible for setting departmental goals, establishing cleaning standards, managing budgets, and coordinating with other hotel departments.
   - The Executive Housekeeper reports directly to the General Manager or Assistant General Manager.

2. **Assistant Executive Housekeeper / Assistant Director of Housekeeping:**

   - The Assistant Executive Housekeeper assists the Executive Housekeeper in overseeing housekeeping operations. This role involves supervising staff, monitoring cleanliness standards, managing inventory, and assisting with training and scheduling.
   - The Assistant Executive Housekeeper reports to the Executive Housekeeper.

3. **Assistant Managers:**

   - The Assistant Manager in hotel housekeeping plays a crucial role in supporting the smooth and efficient operation of the department. They work closely with the Assistant Executive Housekeeper or Director of Housekeeping and take on various responsibilities to ensure that cleaning and maintenance services meet high standards and guest expectations.

4. **Housekeeping Supervisors / Floor Supervisors:**

   - Housekeeping Supervisors are responsible for supervising housekeeping staff on specific floors or areas of the hotel. They ensure that cleaning tasks are completed according to standards, inspect rooms, assign duties, and handle guest requests or complaints related to housekeeping.

- Housekeeping Supervisors report to the Assistant Executive Housekeeper.

5. **Room Attendants / Housekeeping Attendants:**

    - Room Attendants, also known as Housekeeping Attendants, are responsible for cleaning and maintaining guest rooms and bathrooms. They change bed linens, clean surfaces, replenish amenities, and ensure rooms are tidy and well-presented.

    - Room Attendants report to the Housekeeping Supervisors.

6. **Public Area Attendants / Housepersons :**

    - Public Area Attendants, also called Housepersons, are responsible for maintaining the cleanliness of public spaces, such as lobbies, corridors, elevators, and other common areas. They also assist Room Attendants with tasks like delivering supplies and removing trash.

    - Public Area Attendants report to the Housekeeping Supervisors.

Laundry Department:

1. **Laundry Manager/Director of Laundry :**

    - At the top of the hierarchy is the Laundry Manager or Director of Laundry Services. This position oversees the entire laundry department and is responsible for setting departmental goals, managing laundry operations, maintaining quality standards, and coordinating with other hotel departments.

    - The Laundry Manager reports directly to the General Manager or Assistant General Manager.

2. **Laundry Supervisors:**

    - Laundry Supervisors are responsible for overseeing specific areas of the laundry department, such as linen sorting, washing, drying, folding, and delivery.

    - They supervise laundry staff, ensure efficient workflow, monitor equipment maintenance, and handle any issues related to laundry operations.

    - Laundry Supervisors report to the Laundry Manager.

3. **Laundry Attendants:**

   - Laundry Attendants are the frontline staff responsible for the day-to-day laundry operations.

   - They sort, wash, dry, fold, and press hotel linens, towels, and uniforms, ensuring cleanliness and quality standards are met .

   - Laundry Attendants may also be responsible for receiving, storing, and distributing clean linens to other hotel departments.

   - Laundry Attendants report to the Laundry Supervisors.

4. **Pressers / Ironers:**

   - In larger laundry departments, there may be dedicated Pressers or Ironers who specialize in pressing and ironing linens and uniforms to ensure a neat and polished appearance.

   - Pressers may report to the Laundry Supervisors or directly to the Laundry Manager, depending on the size of the laundry department.

Note - The hierarchy may vary in smaller hotels or hotels with smaller laundry operations. In such cases, the Laundry Manager may directly oversee laundry staff without the need for intermediate supervisor positions.

CHAPTER 2
Housekeeping Management

Housekeeping management refers to the management of housekeeping operations in hotels and other hospitality establishments. It involves the planning, organization, staffing, and coordination of housekeeping services to ensure that guest rooms, public areas, and other spaces are clean, comfortable, and safe.

The main functions of housekeeping management include:

1. **Planning and organizing** - Developing policies and procedures for housekeeping operations, setting cleaning schedules, and ensuring that equipment and supplies are available.

1. Planning in Housekeeping:

- **Task Scheduling** - Housekeeping planning starts with creating a well-structured schedule for cleaning tasks. This includes daily routines, weekly deep cleaning, and periodic maintenance activities. The schedule should consider factors like occupancy rate, special events, and peak periods.

- **Staff Allocation** - Allocate the appropriate number of staff members to each task based on workload and expertise. Ensure that the staffing aligns with the occupancy levels, with more staff available during busy times and fewer during quieter periods.

- **Inventory Management** - Plan and maintain an inventory of cleaning supplies, equipment, and guest amenities. This involves predicting the consumption rate and replenishing items before they run out to avoid interruptions in cleaning services.

- **Quality Standards** - Set clear and specific standards for cleanliness and maintenance. Plan for regular quality checks and inspections to ensure that these standards are consistently met and identify areas that may need improvement.

- **Guest Room Management** - Develop a systematic approach to managing guest rooms, including check-in and check-out procedures, room assignments, and coordination with the front desk to ensure a smooth workflow.

2. Organizing in Housekeeping:

- **Task Allocation** - Organize tasks into categories such as guest room cleaning, public area maintenance, laundry, and special requests. Assign specific responsibilities to housekeeping staff based on their skills and expertise.

- **Cleaning Checklists** - Create detailed checklists for each cleaning task to ensure that nothing is overlooked. These checklists outline the tasks, methods, and cleaning agents required for each area or item.

- **Equipment and Supplies** - Organize cleaning equipment and supplies in a central storage area for easy access. Each staff member should have their designated cleaning cart stocked with the necessary tools and products.

- **Linen and Laundry Management** - Organize the laundering process, including sorting, washing, and storing linens. Keep track of linen usage to ensure an adequate supply is available at all times.

- **Waste Management** - Organize waste disposal and recycling processes, with clearly labeled bins in appropriate locations to encourage proper waste segregation.

- **Record Keeping** - Maintain organized records of cleaning schedules, inventory levels, and staff performance. This data helps in assessing housekeeping efficiency and making informed decisions for improvement.

Benefits of Planning & Organizing in Housekeeping:

- **Efficiency** - Planning and organizing ensure that tasks are performed systematically, reducing wasted time and effort.

- **Consistency** - Standardized procedures and checklists lead to consistent and high-quality cleaning outcomes.

- **Guest Satisfaction -** A well-organized housckeeping operation contributes to a clean and comfortable environment, enhancing guest satisfaction and loyalty.

- **Resource Management -** Effective planning and organization lead to optimized resource usage, reducing wastage and lowering operational costs.

- **Workplace Safety -** Organized housekeeping practices contribute to a safer work environment for staff, minimizing accidents and injuries.

Overall, planning and organizing in housekeeping are essential for maintaining cleanliness, order, and guest satisfaction in hotels and other hospitality establishments

2. **Staffing and training** - Recruiting, hiring, and training housekeeping staff, ensuring they have the necessary skills, and providing ongoing training and support.

Staffing and training are crucial aspects of housekeeping, as they directly impact the efficiency, quality, and guest satisfaction of the housekeeping services. Let's delve into each aspect:

1. Staffing in Housekeeping:

- **Determining Staffing Levels -** The first step in staffing is to determine the appropriate number of housekeeping personnel required to manage the hotel's size and occupancy rate. This involves analyzing the number of rooms, public areas, and special requirements to create an optimal staff-to-room ratio.

- **Recruitment and Selection -** Recruiting skilled and dedicated individuals is essential for a successful housekeeping team. Hiring managers should look for candidates with relevant experience, attention to detail, and a positive attitude.

- **Job Descriptions and Roles -** Clearly define the roles and responsibilities of each housekeeping position, such as room attendants, supervisors, housekeeping managers, and laundry staff. This ensures that everyone understands their tasks and contributes effectively to the team.

- **Training and Onboarding -** Provide comprehensive onboarding for new employees, introducing them to the hotel's housekeeping procedures, safety protocols, and service standards.

- **Cross-Training :** Encourage cross-training among housekeeping staff so that they can handle various tasks efficiently. This flexibility allows for better task allocation and contingency planning.

2. Training in Housekeeping:

- **Housekeeping Procedures -** Train staff on standard operating procedures (SOPs) for cleaning and maintaining different areas of the hotel, including guest rooms, public spaces, and back-of-house areas. Emphasize attention to detail and adherence to hygiene standards.

- **Product Knowledge -** Educate housekeeping staff about the correct use of cleaning agents, equipment, and supplies. Proper knowledge ensures effective and safe cleaning practices.

- **Time Management -** Provide training in time management to help staff complete their tasks efficiently without compromising quality.

- **Customer Service Skills -** Housekeeping staff often have direct contact with guests. Training in customer service helps them handle guest requests and complaints professionally and courteously.

- **Health and Safety -** Focus on health and safety training, including proper handling of hazardous materials, safe usage of equipment, and awareness of potential hazards in the work environment. Regularly update staff on new safety protocols and best practices.

- **Communication Skills -** Effective communication among housekeeping staff and with other hotel departments is vital for smooth operations. Training should emphasize clear communication and teamwork.

- **Language Proficiency -** In hotels with international guests, language training may be necessary to ensure effective communication and enhance the guest experience.

Benefits of Staffing & Training in Housekeeping:

- **Improved Service Quality -** Well-trained and motivated staff provide higher-quality cleaning services, leading to increased guest satisfaction.

- **Efficiency and Productivity -** Adequate staffing and proper training result in efficient task completion, reducing operational costs and increasing productivity.
- **Safety Compliance -** Proper training ensures that staff follows safety protocols, reducing the risk of accidents and injuries in the workplace.
- **Employee Morale -** Training and skill development contribute to employee satisfaction and morale, leading to higher staff retention rates.
- **Guest Satisfaction -** A well-trained and attentive housekeeping team creates a positive impression on guests, enhancing their overall experience during their stay.

Investing in staffing and training for housekeeping staff is a worthwhile endeavor that benefits both the hotel and its guests. Well-trained and motivated housekeeping teams play a significant role in maintaining a clean, safe, and comfortable environment for guests, contributing to the overall success of the hotel

3. **Coordination** - Coordinating housekeeping services with other departments such as front office, maintenance, and food and beverage to ensure that guest needs are met.

Coordination in hotel housekeeping refers to the effective synchronization and collaboration among various departments and individuals involved in housekeeping operations. It is essential for ensuring a smooth and seamless flow of activities, leading to efficient cleaning, maintenance, and guest service. Effective coordination ensures that all housekeeping tasks are completed on time and to the expected standards. Here's how coordination works in hotel housekeeping:

1. Interdepartmental Coordination:

- **Front Desk -** The front desk plays a critical role in housekeeping coordination. They communicate the room status to housekeeping, indicating which rooms need cleaning, which are occupied, and which are vacant. Housekeeping, in turn, informs the front desk when rooms are ready for new arrivals.
- **Maintenance -** Housekeeping and maintenance departments need to work closely together, especially when addressing repairs or maintenance issues in guest rooms or public areas. Prompt communication between the two ensures that repairs are done without causing inconvenience to guests.

- **Laundry** - The laundry department collaborates with housekeeping to ensure a steady supply of clean linens and towels. Coordination here is essential to manage the flow of dirty linens and return clean ones efficiently.

2. Task Allocation and Communication:

- **Supervisors and Team Leaders:** Housekeeping supervisors and team leaders play a crucial role in coordinating the activities of housekeeping staff. They assign tasks, monitor progress, and ensure that tasks are completed on time.

- **Cleaning Schedules:** Coordinating cleaning schedules with room occupancy and guest preferences is vital to prevent disturbances and maintain guest satisfaction. Scheduling should consider check-in/check-out times, do-not-disturb requests, and special guest requirements.

3. Communication Tools and Technology:

- **Housekeeping Software** - Many hotels use housekeeping software that allows supervisors to track room status, schedule tasks, and communicate with staff in real-time. This technology streamlines coordination and improves efficiency.

- **Housekeeping Boards and Reports** - Physical or digital housekeeping boards are used to display room statuses, special requests, and important information for staff. Regular reports help assess performance and identify areas for improvement.

4. Emergency Coordination:

- **Emergency Preparedness** - Housekeeping staff should be trained to handle emergency situations such as fire, natural disasters, or medical emergencies. They need to coordinate with other hotel staff and follow established emergency protocols to ensure the safety of guests and colleagues.

5. Training and Teamwork:

- **Team Bonding** - Encouraging teamwork and positive working relationships among housekeeping staff fosters better communication and collaboration during daily operations.

- **Cross -Training:** Cross-training staff in different housekeeping tasks enables greater flexibility and coverage during busy periods or staff shortages.

Benefits of Coordination in Hotel Housekeeping:

- **Efficiency** - Effective coordination optimizes housekeeping operations, leading to better time management and task completion.

- **Guest Satisfaction** - Well-coordinated housekeeping services lead to a clean and comfortable environment for guests, enhancing their overall experience.

- **Resource Management** - Coordinating with other departments and optimizing cleaning schedules helps minimize wastage and unnecessary disruptions.

- **Safety and Emergency Response** - Seamless coordination ensures a prompt response to emergencies and improves overall safety in the hotel.

In conclusion, coordination in hotel housekeeping is vital for delivering exceptional guest experiences and maintaining the overall functionality and cleanliness of the hotel. Effective coordination involves clear communication, proper training, and collaborative efforts among different departments and housekeeping staff.

4. **Budgeting** - Developing and managing budgets for housekeeping operations, including labor, supplies, and equipment. Budgeting in hotel housekeeping involves the process of planning and allocating financial resources to support the efficient and effective management of housekeeping operations. A well-designed budget enables the housekeeping department to deliver high-quality services, maintain cleanliness standards, and meet guest expectations while also controlling costs. Here's how budgeting works in hotel housekeeping:

1. **Expenses and Cost Categories:**

- **Labor Costs** - This includes wages, salaries, benefits, and overtime pay for housekeeping staff. Labor costs typically constitute a significant portion of the housekeeping budget.

- **Cleaning Supplies** - Budgeting for cleaning agents, chemicals, guest amenities, linens, towels, and other consumables needed for daily operations.

- **Equipment and Maintenance** - Allocating funds for the purchase, repair, and maintenance of housekeeping equipment like vacuum cleaners, carpet cleaners, laundry machines, and carts.

- **Training and Development** - Setting aside funds for housekeeping staff training and development programs to enhance their skills and knowledge.

- **Uniforms and Staff Amenities** - Budgeting for uniforms, safety gear, and other amenities provided to housekeeping staff.

- **Outsourcing** - If the hotel contracts third-party cleaning services for specific tasks, budgeting for these external services is necessary.

- **Miscellaneous Expenses** - Allocating funds for unexpected or incidental expenses related to housekeeping operations.

2. Forecasting and Planning:

- Housekeeping budgeting typically involves analyzing historical data, occupancy rates, guest trends, and seasonal variations to make informed projections for future expenses.

- Forecasting allows housekeeping managers to anticipate periods of high demand (e.g., peak tourist seasons) and allocate resources accordingly.

3. Setting Budget Targets:

- Based on the forecasted expenses and revenue projections, housekeeping managers set budget targets for each cost category.

- Targets should be realistic and align with the overall financial goals of the hotel.

4. Cost Control and Monitoring:

- Throughout the budgeting period, housekeeping managers need to monitor actual expenses regularly and compare them to the budget targets.

- Cost control measures may be implemented to stay within budget, such as finding cost-effective suppliers, reducing waste, or optimizing staff scheduling.

5. Flexibility and Contingency:

- The budget should allow for some flexibility to accommodate unforeseen changes or emergencies that may affect housekeeping operations.

- Contingency planning ensures the department is prepared to handle unexpected events that could impact the budget.

6. Collaboration with Other Departments:

- Housekeeping managers need to collaborate with other departments, such as the front desk and procurement, to ensure effective cost management and avoid redundancies.

Benefits of Budgeting in Hotel Housekeeping:

- **Cost Management** - A well-planned budget helps control costs and prevents overspending in housekeeping operations.

- **Resource Allocation** - It ensures that financial resources are allocated appropriately, focusing on areas critical to maintaining cleanliness and guest satisfaction.

- **Performance Evaluation** - Budget targets serve as benchmarks for evaluating the performance of the housekeeping department.

- **Guest Satisfaction** - Adequate budgeting contributes to maintaining high cleanliness standards and guest satisfaction levels.

- **Strategic Planning** - Budgeting facilitates strategic planning, allowing the department to align its goals with the overall objectives of the hotel.

In conclusion, budgeting in hotel housekeeping is a strategic process that involves careful planning, forecasting, and cost control. By allocating financial resources efficiently, the housekeeping department can maintain cleanliness standards, deliver exceptional guest experiences, and contribute to the overall success of the hotel.

5. **Quality control** - Ensuring that housekeeping services meet established standards for cleanliness, safety, and guest satisfaction.

Quality control in hotel housekeeping is a systematic process that ensures the delivery of consistent and high-quality cleaning and maintenance services throughout the hotel. It involves setting and maintaining high standards, regular inspections, and corrective actions to achieve guest satisfaction and uphold the hotel's reputation. Here's how quality control is implemented in hotel housekeeping:

1. Setting Quality Standards:

- Clearly define the cleaning and maintenance standards that housekeeping staff must adhere to. This includes expectations for room cleanliness, public area maintenance, linen quality, and overall presentation.

- Establishing specific benchmarks and measurable metrics allows for objective evaluation and improvement.

2. Standard Operating Procedures (SOPs):

- Develop detailed SOPs for each housekeeping task, outlining step-by-step instructions for cleaning different areas and items. SOPs help maintain consistency in service delivery.

- Ensure that all staff members are trained on these procedures and follow them rigorously.

3. Inspection and Evaluation:

- Regularly conduct inspections of guest rooms, public areas, and back-of-house spaces to assess the quality of cleaning and maintenance.

- Inspections can be conducted by housekeeping supervisors, managers, or designated quality control personnel.

- Use checklists or digital tools to record inspection findings and identify areas for improvement.

4. Guest Feedback:

- Guest feedback is a valuable tool for quality control. Encourage guests to provide feedback on housekeeping services through surveys or comment cards.

- Monitor guest reviews and address any concerns or complaints related to housekeeping promptly.

5. Corrective Actions and Training:

- When quality issues are identified, take immediate corrective actions to rectify the situation. This may involve re-cleaning, addressing maintenance issues, or replacing items.

- If recurring issues arise, provide additional training or refresher courses for housekeeping staff to improve their skills and knowledge.

6. Team Motivation and Recognition:

- Motivated staff are more likely to deliver high-quality services. Recognize and reward housekeeping employees for their efforts and achievements.
- Promote a culture of excellence and continuous improvement within the housekeeping team.

7. Use of Technology:

- Utilize technology to aid in quality control, such as housekeeping management software that tracks room status, inspections, and task completion.
- Digital tools can streamline communication and ensure that information is readily available to all relevant staff.

8. Collaboration with Other Departments:

- Housekeeping should collaborate with other hotel departments, particularly the front desk, to ensure smooth communication and resolve any guest-related issues promptly.

Benefits of Quality Control in Hotel Housekeeping:

- **Guest Satisfaction:** Ensuring high-quality housekeeping services contributes to positive guest experiences and satisfaction.
- **Brand Reputation:** Consistent quality control helps build a strong reputation for the hotel as a clean and well-maintained establishment.
- **Operational Efficiency:** Quality control measures streamline housekeeping operations and reduce wastage, leading to better resource management.
- **Staff Performance:** Monitoring and improving quality motivates staff to perform better and take pride in their work.
- **Guest Loyalty:** Satisfied guests are more likely to become repeat customers and recommend the hotel to others.

In summary, quality control in hotel housekeeping is vital for maintaining a clean and well-maintained environment that meets guests' expectations and enhances their overall experience. By setting and maintaining high standards, regularly inspecting and evaluating performance, and implementing corrective actions, hotels can ensure that their housekeeping services consistently meet or exceed guest expectations.

Staffing and training housekeeping staff in hotels is crucial to ensure that they provide high-quality housekeeping services that meet guest expectations. Here are some important considerations for staffing and training housekeeping staff in hotels:

1. **Recruitment and selection** - Hire candidates with the necessary qualifications, experience, and personal attributes to excel in housekeeping roles. Ensure that the recruitment process includes thorough background checks and references.

2. **On-boarding** - Provide new staff with a comprehensive orientation that covers the hotel's policies, procedures, and service standards. This should also include job-specific training on cleaning techniques, chemical handling, and equipment operation.

3. **Ongoing training** - Provide regular training sessions to help staff develop their skills and keep up to date with new cleaning technologies and techniques. This could include classroom instruction, on-the-job training, or external training courses.

4. **Cross-training** - Cross-train staff to perform different housekeeping functions, such as cleaning guest rooms, public areas, or laundry operations. This can help to ensure that there is sufficient coverage during peak periods and reduce reliance on temporary staff.

5. **Performance management** - Develop performance metrics and review processes to help staff understand how they are performing and where they can improve. This could include regular performance appraisals, goal-setting, and feedback sessions.

6. **Career development** - Provide staff with opportunities for career development, such as mentoring programs, skills development, and promotions. This can help to improve staff retention and motivation.

By investing in the recruitment, onboarding, training, and development of housekeeping staff, hotels can create a highly skilled and motivated team that can deliver exceptional housekeeping services to guests. This can help to improve guest satisfaction, reduce turnover, and promote a positive image of the hotel.

CHAPTER 3
Cleaning Techniques & Equipments

Hotels use a variety of cleaning tools and equipment to ensure that their rooms and common areas are kept clean and well-maintained. The following are some of the most commonly used cleaning tools in hotels:

1. **Vacuum cleaner** - A vacuum cleaner is used to remove dirt and debris from carpets and floors in hotel rooms and common areas.

2. **Mop and bucket** - Mops and buckets are used to clean floors, especially in areas where vacuuming is not possible or effective, such as in bathrooms or kitchens.

3. **Microfiber cloths** - Microfiber cloths are highly effective for cleaning surfaces such as mirrors, windows, and countertops, as they are gentle on surfaces and can absorb dirt and dust effectively.

4. **Cleaning solutions** - Hotels use a variety of cleaning solutions, including all-purpose cleaners, disinfectants, and stain removers, to clean surfaces and remove stains.

5. **Scrub brushes** - Scrub brushes are used to remove stubborn stains or grime from surfaces, especially in areas such as bathrooms or kitchens.

6. **Dusters** - Dusters are used to remove dust and cobwebs from hard-to-reach areas, such as high ceilings, light fixtures, and corners.

7. **Trash cans and liners** - Trash cans and liners are used to collect and dispose of waste in hotel rooms and common areas.

8. **Floor Scrubbers** - These machines are used to scrub and clean large areas of hard floors. They have rotating brushes or pads that remove dirt and stains from the floor surface.

9. **Carpet Extractors** - These machines are specifically designed to deep clean carpets by injecting water and cleaning solution into the carpet fibers and then extracting the dirty water. They help remove stains, dirt, and odors from carpets.

10. **Steam Cleaners** - Steam cleaning equipment uses high-temperature steam to clean and sanitize various surfaces, including upholstery, curtains, mattresses, and bathroom fixtures.

11. **Pressure Washers** - These machines use high-pressure water spray to remove stubborn dirt, grime, and mold from outdoor surfaces like walkways, patios, and building exteriors.

12. **Window Cleaning Equipment** - This includes tools like squeegees, extension poles, and window cleaning solutions to clean windows and glass surfaces in hotel rooms and public areas.

13. **Wet and Dry Vacuums** - These versatile vacuums can handle both wet and dry debris, making them useful for cleaning spills and wet areas in hotel bathrooms, kitchens, and other areas.

Overall, the use of the right cleaning tools and equipment is essential for maintaining high cleanliness standards in hotels. Effective cleaning can help to create a safe, healthy, and welcoming environment for guests and staff alike.

Cleaning Techniques

Housekeeping cleaning techniques involve a combination of methods and procedures to efficiently and effectively clean various areas and items in a hotel or other hospitality establishment. These techniques are designed to achieve high levels of cleanliness, hygiene, and guest satisfaction. Here are some common cleaning techniques used in housekeeping:

1. Surface Cleaning:

- **Dusting:** Using dry or damp microfiber cloths, dust all surfaces, including furniture, fixtures, and decorative items, to remove dust and debris.
- **Polishing:** Use appropriate polishing agents to shine and restore the luster of surfaces like glass, mirrors, metal fittings, and wood furniture.

- **Spot Cleaning:** Quickly address spills and stains on surfaces and carpets to prevent them from becoming more challenging to remove later.

2. Room Cleaning:

- **Bed Making:** Strip and remake beds with fresh linens and ensure proper alignment and tucking for a neat appearance.

- **Bathroom Cleaning:** Clean and disinfect bathroom fixtures, such as sinks, toilets, bathtubs, and showers. Pay special attention to high-touch areas.

- **Vacuuming and Mopping :** Thoroughly vacuum carpets and mop hard floors using appropriate cleaning agents to remove dirt and stains.

3. Public Area Cleaning:

- **Lobby and Reception Cleaning:** Maintain the lobby's appearance by cleaning furniture, sweeping and mopping floors, and ensuring the front desk is tidy.

- **Corridor Cleaning:** Vacuum and mop corridors regularly, paying attention to corners and baseboards.

- **Elevator Cleaning:** Wipe down elevator buttons, handrails, and interior surfaces frequently to maintain hygiene.

4. Back-of-House Cleaning:

- **Staff Areas:** Regularly clean staff break rooms, locker rooms, and offices to maintain a clean and comfortable environment for employees.

- **Housekeeping Storage Areas:** Keep housekeeping storage areas organized and clean to ensure quick access to supplies and equipment.

5. Specialized Cleaning Techniques:

- **Carpet Shampooing:** Periodically deep clean carpets using carpet cleaning machines or professional services to remove embedded dirt and stains.

- **Upholstery Cleaning:** Use appropriate techniques and equipment to clean upholstery and fabric-covered furniture.

- **Window Cleaning:** Clean windows and glass surfaces using appropriate cleaning agents and tools for streak-free results.

- **Deep Cleaning:** Conduct thorough deep cleaning on a regular basis to address hard-to-reach and often overlooked areas.

6. Green Cleaning:

- Many housekeeping departments now adopt environmentally friendly cleaning techniques that use eco-friendly cleaning products and minimize water and energy usage.

7. Cleaning Tools and Equipment:

- Housekeeping staff use various tools and equipment, including vacuum cleaners, mops, microfiber cloths, dusters, scrub brushes, and cleaning carts, to perform their tasks efficiently.

8. Infection Control:

- In light of health concerns like COVID-19, housekeeping teams may implement additional infection control measures, such as using disinfectants on high-touch surfaces and frequently sanitizing common areas.

Safety Considerations:

- Housekeeping staff should follow safety protocols, such as wearing appropriate personal protective equipment (PPE) and handling cleaning chemicals safely.

Training and Supervision:

- Proper training and regular supervision ensure that housekeeping staff are proficient in using cleaning techniques and adhere to quality standards.

By implementing these cleaning techniques, the housekeeping department can maintain a clean, hygienic, and inviting environment for guests, leading to higher guest satisfaction and loyalty.

Overall, the use of effective cleaning techniques is essential for maintaining high cleanliness standards in hotels. Using the right techniques can help to create a safe, healthy, and welcoming environment for guests and staff.

STAS Group
Since 1986

STAS - Is one of the leading brands in chemical manufacturing in INDIA, with a wide experience pool of over 35 years in chemical designing and manufacturing, strong PAN INDIA Presence and having a patronage of thousands of clients across 3 countries, 15 states and 70 cities and counting ...

At STAS we have complete range of international standard products for Housekeeping, kitchen care, dry cleaning, retail Laundry, wet cleaning, Commercial Laundry and kitchen care for hotels and hospitals. Our product range is time tested and authentic. We strictly adhere to various quality control measures and ensure that the final product is of top quality, best in class, most effective and result oriented.

We cherish a strong position as the most favourite and trusted Vendor amongst our clientele, for not only providing best in class product, services and technical support but also for developing tailor made solutions for their specific demands.
At STAS GROUP we endeavour to achieve total customer satisfaction through superior products, quality, services and innovations. To ensure that the trust in our quality is never betrayed, we are focusing on consistent quality products to provide top most quality products to our customers who have shown immense confidence in our range of products.

Here at STAS GROUP our vision emphasis on the feedback and knowledge of the customers and create and deliver the best using the available human resources and technology.

Our Brands :

STASROM :
Range of Housekeeping Chemicals, like Surface cleaner, surface sanitizers, Marble / steel / wood polish, air fresheners, Speciality products etc.

STASH :
Complete range of Linen Care / Laundry Chemicals. Dedicated range for Hotels and Hospitals, with stain removers and fabric conditioners.

STASDISH :
Complete range of kitchen care Chemicals, like dish washers, Surface cleaner, surface sanitizers, degreasers, etc

For any requirement / <u>free demonstrations</u> or enquiry please feel to contact us.
We are also open for channel partners from all across the globe.

Mob : +91-9910089225 , +91-9810484225
Email : info@staschemgroup.com
Website : www.staschemgroup.com

CHAPTER 4
Room Cleaning Procedures

Room cleaning procedures are vitally important in hotels for several reasons:

1. **Guest Satisfaction:** Clean and well-maintained rooms lead to higher guest satisfaction. When guests check into a clean and tidy room, they are more likely to have a positive impression of the hotel and enjoy their stay. This, in turn, can lead to positive reviews, repeat business, and word-of-mouth recommendations.

2. **Health and Safety:** Cleanliness is crucial for maintaining a healthy and safe environment for guests. Proper cleaning procedures help prevent the spread of germs and bacteria, reducing the risk of guests falling ill during their stay. It also helps control pests, allergens, and other potential health hazards.

3. **Brand Reputation:** A hotel's reputation is a crucial factor in attracting guests. Positive reviews and recommendations from satisfied guests contribute to a hotel's brand reputation. On the other hand, negative reviews related to cleanliness issues can significantly damage a hotel's image and affect its business.

4. **Compliance with Regulations:** Hotels are subject to various health and safety regulations, including cleanliness standards. Following proper room cleaning procedures ensures that the hotel stays compliant with these regulations and avoids any penalties or legal issues.

5. **Guest Loyalty:** Guests are more likely to become loyal customers if they consistently have positive experiences during their stays. A clean and well-maintained room contributes to a positive experience, increasing the chances of guests returning to the hotel in the future.

6. **Enhanced Guest Experience:** A clean and organized room enhances the overall guest experience. When guests enter a room that is well-prepared and free from clutter, they feel more comfortable and relaxed, which can elevate their entire stay.

7. **Efficient Operations:** Standardized cleaning procedures help streamline the housekeeping process, making it more efficient and organized. This allows housekeeping staff to manage their tasks effectively, leading to quicker room turnaround times and better overall operations.

8. **Employee Satisfaction:** A well-structured cleaning process provides clear guidelines and expectations for housekeeping staff. When employees know what is expected of them and have the necessary tools and resources, it can lead to higher job satisfaction and productivity.

9. **Sustainability:** Many hotels are adopting eco-friendly cleaning practices to reduce their environmental impact. Proper cleaning procedures, such as using green cleaning products and efficient water and energy usage, contribute to the hotel's sustainability initiatives.

10. **Preventive Maintenance:** Regular cleaning and maintenance of rooms can help identify and address minor issues before they escalate into major problems. This proactive approach can save the hotel time and money in the long run.

In summary, room cleaning procedures are essential in hotels because they directly impact guest satisfaction, health and safety, brand reputation, and overall operational efficiency. A well-maintained and clean environment is a key factor in ensuring guests have a pleasant and enjoyable stay, leading to a successful and thriving hospitality business.

Departure Room Cleaning Procedure

The departure room service procedure in a hotel room involves a series of steps that housekeeping staff follows to ensure that the room is cleaned and prepared for the next guest. The following is an overview of the departure room service procedure:

1. **Knock and announce** - Housekeeping staff knocks on the door and announces themselves as "housekeeping" before entering the room. This is done to ensure that the guest is aware of their presence and privacy is respected.

2. **Empty the trash** - Housekeeping staff first empties all trash cans in the room and replaces the trash liners.

3. **Stripping the beds** - The housekeeping staff removes all used bedding, including sheets, pillowcases, and duvet covers. The used bedding is then taken to the laundry room for cleaning.

4. **Cleaning the bathroom** - The bathroom is then cleaned thoroughly, including the toilet, sink, shower, and bathtub. Housekeeping staff also restocks the bathroom with fresh towels, toilet paper, and other amenities.

5. **Cleaning the bedroom** - The bedroom is then cleaned thoroughly, including dusting and vacuuming, and wiping down all surfaces, such as tables, dressers, and nightstands.

6. **Check for lost and found items** - Housekeeping staff checks the room for any lost and found items that may have been left by the previous guest.

7. **Restocking the room** - The room is then restocked with fresh linens, towels, and other amenities, such as shampoo, soap, and coffee supplies.

8. **Final inspection** - The housekeeping staff performs a final inspection to ensure that the room is clean, organized, and ready for the next guest.

9. **Report any damages or maintenance issues** - Any damages or maintenance issues found during the cleaning process are reported to the maintenance staff or hotel management for prompt attention.

Overall, the departure room service procedure is a critical step in maintaining a clean and comfortable environment for hotel guests. By following a standardized procedure, the housekeeping staff can ensure that the room is cleaned efficiently and effectively, leaving the guest with a positive impression of their stay.

Stayover Room Cleaning Procedure

The occupied or stayover room service procedure in a hotel room is designed to refresh and tidy the room while the guest is still occupying it. The following is an overview of the occupied or stayover room service procedure:

1. **Knock and announce** - Housekeeping staff knocks on the door and announces themselves as "housekeeping" before entering the room. This is done to ensure that the guest is aware of their presence and privacy is respected.

2. **Empty trash and replace liners** - Housekeeping staff first empties all trash cans in the room and replaces the liners.

3. **Tidy up -** Housekeeping staff tidies up the room, which includes making the bed, fluffing pillows, straightening up furniture, and picking up any clutter.

4. **Cleaning the bathroom -** The bathroom is then cleaned thoroughly, including the toilet, sink, shower, and bathtub. Housekeeping staff also restocks the bathroom with fresh towels, toilet paper, and other amenities.

5. **Cleaning the bedroom** - The bedroom is then cleaned thoroughly, including dusting and vacuuming, and wiping down all surfaces, such as tables, dressers, and nightstands.

6. **Check for supplies** - Housekeeping staff checks to ensure that the guest has an adequate supply of fresh linens, towels, and other amenities, such as shampoo, soap, and coffee supplies.

7. **Refresh amenities** - If the guest's amenities, such as coffee supplies, have been used up, housekeeping staff replenishes them as needed.

8. **Final inspection** - The housekeeping staff performs a final inspection to ensure that the room is clean, organized, and ready for the guest's continued occupancy.

9. **Report any damages or maintenance issues** - Any damages or maintenance issues found during the cleaning process are reported to the maintenance staff or hotel management for prompt attention.

Overall, the occupied or stayover room service procedure is designed to provide the guest with a clean and comfortable environment while they continue to occupy the room. By following a standardized procedure, the housekeeping staff can efficiently and effectively refresh the room, leaving the guest with a positive impression of their stay.

Bed Making Procedure

Hotel bed making is a critical aspect of housekeeping, as it ensures that the guest has a comfortable and clean place to sleep. The following is a general procedure for making a bed in a hotel:

1. **Strip the bed** - Remove all the used bedding, including the sheets, pillowcases, and duvet covers.

2. **Inspect the mattress and pillows** - Check the mattress and pillows for any stains or signs of wear and tear. If any issues are found, report them to the hotel maintenance staff.

3. **Fit the bottom sheet** - Start by fitting a fresh bottom sheet over the mattress, ensuring that it's tucked in tightly and smoothly.

4. **Add the top sheet** - Place a fresh top sheet over the bottom sheet, ensuring that the sheet is even on both sides and at the bottom of the bed.

5. **Tuck in the sides** - Tuck in the sides of the top sheet and bottom sheet at the foot of the bed, ensuring that the sheets are snug and tight.

6. **Add the duvet or comforter** - Place a fresh duvet or comforter over the sheets, ensuring that it's evenly distributed on both sides.

7. **Arrange pillows** - Place two fresh pillows at the head of the bed, standing them up against the headboard.

8. **Add pillowcases** - Place fresh pillowcases over the pillows, ensuring that the openings face away from the center of the bed.

9. **Add additional blankets or throws** - If the hotel provides additional blankets or throws, place them at the foot of the bed for the guest's convenience.

10. **Final touches** - Smooth out any wrinkles in the bedding and ensure that the bed is clean and tidy.

Overall, following a standardized bed making procedure is essential in ensuring that the guest has a clean and comfortable place to sleep during their stay in the hotel.

WC Cleaning Procedure

Cleaning a toilet or a WC is an important task in hotel housekeeping to ensure that guests have a clean and hygienic bathroom. Here is a general procedure for cleaning a toilet:

1. **Gather cleaning supplies** - Before starting, gather all necessary cleaning supplies, such as gloves, a toilet brush, cleaning solution, disinfectant, and a scrub pad.

2. **Put on gloves** - Put on gloves to protect your hands from germs and bacteria.

3. **Flush the toilet** - Flush the toilet to remove any waste and debris.

4. **Apply cleaning solution** - Apply a cleaning solution to the inside of the bowl, including the rim, seat, and lid.

5. **Scrub the bowl** - Use a toilet brush to scrub the inside of the bowl thoroughly, paying special attention to the area under the rim and any stains.

6. **Clean the seat and lid** - Use a disinfectant solution to clean the seat and lid, wiping down the entire surface with a scrub pad.

7. **Clean the exterior** - Use a disinfectant solution and scrub pad to clean the exterior of the toilet, including the tank, base, and handle.

8. **Wipe down surfaces** - Use a disinfectant solution and a clean cloth to wipe down all surfaces, including the toilet paper dispenser and any other fixtures.

9. **Mop the floor** - After cleaning the toilet, mop the floor around the toilet with a disinfectant solution to ensure that any germs or bacteria are eliminated.

10. **Restock supplies** - Finally, check to make sure that all supplies, such as toilet paper, soap, and paper towels, are fully stocked and readily available for the guest.

Overall, following a standardized toilet cleaning procedure is essential in ensuring that the bathroom is clean and hygienic for the guests. This not only enhances their experience but also helps prevent the spread of germs and bacteria.

Bathroom Cleaning Procedure

Cleaning a hotel bathroom is an important task in housekeeping, as it ensures that guests have a clean and hygienic environment to use during their stay. Here is a general procedure for cleaning a hotel bathroom:

1. **Gather cleaning supplies** - Before starting, gather all necessary cleaning supplies, such as gloves, cleaning solution, disinfectant, scrub pads, sponges, and a bucket.

2. **Remove all used towels and linens** - Collect all used towels and linens, and replace them with fresh ones.

3. **Remove any trash** - Empty the trash cans and replace the liners as necessary.

4. **Clean the shower or bathtub** - Spray the shower or bathtub with cleaning solution, and scrub the surface with a scrub pad or sponge. Rinse thoroughly with water, and wipe down the surface with a clean cloth.

5. **Clean the sink** - Spray the sink with cleaning solution, and scrub the surface with a scrub pad or sponge. Rinse thoroughly with water, and wipe down the surface with a clean cloth.

6. **Clean the toilet** - Follow the WC cleaning procedure mentioned earlier to thoroughly clean and disinfect the toilet.

7. **Clean the mirrors and surfaces** - Spray mirrors and other surfaces, such as countertops and tiles, with cleaning solution, and wipe down with a clean cloth.

8. **Mop the floor** - After cleaning all surfaces, mop the floor with a disinfectant solution, paying special attention to any corners and edges.

9. **Restock supplies** - Check to make sure that all supplies, such as toilet paper, soap, and towels, are fully stocked and readily available for the guest.

Overall, following a standardized bathroom cleaning procedure is essential in ensuring that the guest bathroom is clean and hygienic. This not only enhances their experience but also helps prevent the spread of germs and bacteria.

Turndown Service Procedure

The turndown service is an important aspect of hotel housekeeping, providing an extra touch of comfort and attention to detail for guests in the evening. Here's a typical hotel housekeeping turndown procedure:

1. **Gather necessary supplies** - The housekeeping staff should collect the required supplies, such as fresh linens (including sheets, pillowcases, and duvet covers), additional amenities like bottled water or chocolates, cleaning cloths, and any special items the hotel provides for turndown service.

2. **Knock and announce** - Before entering the room, the housekeeping staff should knock on the door and announce themselves as "Housekeeping" or "Turndown service."

3. **Enter with caution** - If there's no response from inside the room, the housekeeper should proceed with caution and enter the room gently.

4. **Adjust lighting** - The housekeeper should adjust the lighting in the room to create a relaxing and cozy atmosphere. Typically, this means turning on bedside lamps and dimming or turning off main overhead lights.

5. **Close curtains/blinds** - If the curtains or blinds were opened during the day, the housekeeper should close them to provide privacy and create a soothing ambiance.

6. **Freshen up the room** - Ensure the room is tidy and neat. Remove any used towels, trash, or discarded items from the room.

7. **Make the bed** - Strip any used or wrinkled bed linens and replace them with fresh, clean linens. Make the bed neatly and appropriately, ensuring the sheets are crisp, and the pillows are fluffed.

8. **Turn down the bed** - This involves folding the top sheet and duvet or blanket down to create an inviting and comfortable appearance for the bed. Some hotels may also place a chocolate or a small treat on the pillows as part of the turndown service.

9. **Arrange amenities** - Place fresh towels, bottled water, or any other complimentary items on the bedside table or a designated area.

10. **Check the bathroom** - Ensure the bathroom is clean and well-stocked with fresh towels and toiletries. Restock any necessary items such as toilet paper, shampoo, soap, etc.

11. **Replenish amenities** - Some hotels offer additional amenities, such as slippers, robes, or a turndown card with weather forecasts or a bedtime quote. These should be placed in the room if applicable.

12. **Check for personal items** - Avoid touching or moving any personal items of the guests during the turndown service, unless necessary to tidy up or perform the service.

13. **Leave a turndown card** - If the hotel uses turndown cards, place one on the bedside table with a personalized message or a bedtime quote.

14. **Exit discreetly** - Once the turndown service is complete, leave the room quietly, ensuring the guest's privacy is respected.

Remember that the specific turndown procedure can vary between hotels based on their standards and offerings. The primary goal is to provide a thoughtful and personalized experience for each guest during their stay.

CHAPTER 5
Laundry Services

Laundry service is an important aspect of hotel housekeeping, as guests expect to have access to clean and fresh linens during their stay. Here is a general procedure for laundry service in hotels:

1. **Collect dirty laundry** - Housekeeping staff collects dirty linens and clothes from guest rooms, such as bed sheets, pillowcases, towels, bathrobes, and clothes.

2. **Sort laundry** - Staff sort laundry according to colour, fabric, and level of soiling. This ensures that delicate items are not damaged and that whites remain bright.

3. **Pre-treat stains** - Staff pre-treat any stains on the linens before washing them to ensure they are fully removed.

4. **Load washing machines** - Once sorted, the linens are loaded into washing machines and washed with detergent and fabric softener.

5. **Dry linens** - After washing, the linens are dried in a dryer or hung on a clothesline to air dry.

6. **Fold and iron** - Once dry, the linens are folded or ironed, depending on the hotel's policy, to ensure they look neat and tidy for use in the guest rooms.

7. **Deliver clean linens** - Staff then deliver clean linens to the guest rooms, restocking the beds with fresh sheets and pillowcases and replacing towels as necessary.

8. **Monitor inventory** - Housekeeping staff monitor the inventory of clean linens and towels to ensure that they are fully stocked and readily available for guests.

Overall, laundry service is a critical component of hotel housekeeping. Guests expect clean and fresh linens during their stay, and ensuring that this service is performed to a high standard is essential in providing a positive guest experience.

The process of washing in a hotel laundry typically involves the following steps:

1. **Sorting** - Dirty laundry is sorted according to colour, fabric, and level of soiling. This ensures that delicate items are not damaged, and whites remain bright.

2. **Pre-treatment** - Any stains on the linens are pre-treated with a stain remover before washing.

3. **Loading** - The sorted laundry is loaded into the washing machine.

4. **Detergent and Fabric Softener** - The appropriate amount of detergent and fabric softener is added to the washing machine, according to the type and amount of laundry.

5. **Water temperature** - The water temperature is set based on the type of fabric and level of soiling.

6. **Wash cycle** - The washing machine is set to the appropriate wash cycle based on the type of fabric and level of soiling.

7. **Rinsing** - The laundry is rinsed thoroughly to remove all traces of detergent and fabric softener.

8. **Spinning** - The washing machine spins the laundry to remove excess water.

9. **Drying** - The laundry is dried in a dryer or hung on a clothesline to air dry.

10. **Folding and Ironing** - Once dry, the linens are folded or ironed, depending on the hotel's policy, to ensure they look neat and tidy for use in the guest rooms.

11. **Delivery** - The clean laundry is then delivered to the guest rooms, restocking the beds with fresh sheets and pillowcases and replacing towels as necessary.

Overall, the process of washing in a hotel laundry requires attention to detail and the use of appropriate products and techniques to ensure that the linens are cleaned to a high standard.

The process of drying in a hotel laundry typically involves the following steps:

1. **Loading** - Clean laundry is loaded into the dryer according to the machine's capacity and the type of fabric.

2. **Drying temperature** - The appropriate drying temperature is set based on the type of fabric.

3. **Time** - The drying time is set based on the amount of laundry and the desired level of dryness.

4. **Tumbling** - The dryer tumbles the laundry to prevent wrinkles and ensure even drying.

5. **Checking for dryness** - A housekeeping staff member periodically checks the laundry to ensure that it is not over-dried, which can damage the fabric.

6. **Folding and Ironing** - Once the laundry is dry, it is either folded or ironed, depending on the hotel's policy and the type of fabric.

7. **Delivery** - The clean laundry is then delivered to the guest rooms, restocking the beds with fresh sheets and pillowcases and replacing towels as necessary.

Overall, the process of drying in a hotel laundry requires attention to detail and the use of appropriate temperature settings to prevent damage to the fabric. Regular checking of the laundry during the drying process is also important to ensure that the linens are not over-dried or under-dried, which can affect their quality and appearance.

Dry cleaning is a specialized laundry process that is used to clean delicate fabrics, such as silk, wool, and cashmere, as well as garments that cannot be washed with water. The process of dry cleaning in a hotel laundry typically involves the following steps:

1. **Tagging** - Each item to be dry cleaned is tagged with a unique identification number to ensure that it can be tracked throughout the cleaning process.

2. **Inspection** - The items are inspected for stains and other damage, and any necessary repairs or pre-treatment of stains are done before the dry cleaning process begins.

3. **Loading** - The items are loaded into a specialized dry cleaning machine that uses a chemical solvent, such as perchloroethylene, to clean the fabric.

4. **Cleaning** - The machine agitates the fabric in the solvent, which loosens and removes dirt and stains.

5. **Rinsing** - The solvent is then drained from the machine, and the items are rinsed with a fresh solvent to remove any remaining dirt and detergent.

6. **Drying** - The items are then dried in the machine at a low temperature, which evaporates the solvent and removes any remaining moisture.

7. **Inspection and Finishing** - The items are inspected for any remaining stains or damage and are then pressed, steamed, and finished to ensure that they look their best.

8. **Packaging** - The clean, dry items are then packaged and labelled with their identification numbers, ready for return to the guest.

Overall, the dry cleaning process in a hotel laundry requires specialized equipment and chemicals to ensure that delicate fabrics are cleaned thoroughly without causing damage or shrinkage. Attention to detail and quality control are essential to ensure that the items are returned to the guest in the best possible condition.

Handling guest laundry requests in hotels requires attention to detail and a focus on providing quality service to guests. The following steps can be taken to ensure that guest laundry requests are handled efficiently and effectively:

1. **Guest Laundry Request Form** - Provide a guest laundry request form in the guest room or at the front desk where guests can indicate the items they want laundered, any special instructions, and the preferred delivery time.

2. **Laundry Pickup** - Arrange for housekeeping staff to pick up the laundry from the guest room at the designated time.

3. **Pre-treatment** - Inspect the laundry for stains and pre-treat any stains with appropriate stain-removal products.

4. **Sorting** - Sort the laundry by colour, fabric type, and washing instructions to ensure that each item is laundered appropriately.

5. **Laundering** - Use appropriate washing techniques, detergents, and temperature settings to clean the laundry effectively and without damage.

6. **Drying** - Use appropriate drying techniques and temperature settings to ensure that the laundry is dried thoroughly and without damage.

7. **Folding and Packaging** - Once the laundry is dry, fold it neatly and package it in a laundry bag, along with a copy of the guest's laundry request form.

8. **Delivery** - Deliver the clean laundry to the guest's room at the designated time.

9. **Payment** - Charge the guest's room account for the laundry service or collect payment at the time of delivery, depending on the hotel's policy.

10. **Follow-Up** - Follow up with the guest to ensure that the laundry has been delivered satisfactorily and to address any concerns or issues that may arise.

Overall, handling guest laundry requests in hotels requires attention to detail, effective communication with guests, and a focus on providing quality service. By following these steps, hotels can ensure that guest laundry requests are handled efficiently and effectively, contributing to a positive guest experience.

Hotel laundry facilities require a range of equipment and machines to effectively handle the laundry needs of a large establishment. Here are some common types of laundry equipment and machines used in hotels:

1. **Commercial Washers** - Commercial-grade washing machines are designed to handle high-capacity loads and heavy usage. They come in various sizes, including front-loading and top-loading models, and offer different programmable settings for water temperature, cycle duration, and agitation levels. Some models also feature advanced technology for water and energy efficiency.

2. **Commercial Dryers** - Commercial dryers are specifically designed to dry large quantities of laundry quickly and efficiently. They come in different capacities and can accommodate various types of fabrics. These dryers often feature programmable settings for temperature, time, and moisture sensing to prevent over-drying.

3. **Flatwork Ironers** - Flatwork ironers are used to press and iron large items such as bedsheets, tablecloths, and napkins. They have a continuous feed system that passes the linen through heated rollers, creating a smooth and wrinkle-free finish.

4. **Steam Presses** - Steam presses are used to press smaller items like shirts, trousers, and uniforms. They provide a large surface area for pressing garments with steam and pressure, resulting in crisp and professional-looking clothing.

5. **Dry Cleaning Machines** - Hotels may have on-site dry cleaning equipment for handling delicate fabrics and garments that require specialized cleaning. Dry cleaning machines use non-water-based solvents to remove stains and clean clothes, providing a professional dry cleaning service for guests.

6. **Folding Machines** - Folding machines are used to automate the folding process of items such as towels, bedsheets, and table linens. They save time and ensure consistent folding quality and neatness.

7. **Laundry Carts and Trolleys** - Laundry carts and trolleys are essential for transporting soiled and clean linens throughout the hotel. They are designed to be durable, easy to manoeuver, and equipped with dividers or compartments for organizing different types of laundry .

8. **Laundry Supplies and Accessories** - In addition to machines, hotels require various laundry supplies and accessories such as detergents, fabric softeners, stain removers, laundry bags, hangers, and garment tags. These items contribute to the efficient and effective operation of the hotel's laundry facility.

It's important for hotels to invest in high-quality and reliable laundry equipment that can handle the demands of a large-scale operation. Regular maintenance and servicing of the machines are also crucial to ensure their longevity and optimal performance.

CHAPTER 6
Linen & Uniform Room

A uniform room in hotels is a designated area where hotel staff members, such as housekeeping and front desk personnel, can store and organize their uniforms. It is typically a secure and controlled space where clean uniforms are stored and accessed by staff members as needed.

The purpose of a uniform room is to ensure that hotel employees have access to clean, well-maintained uniforms that adhere to the hotel's dress code and brand standards. It helps maintain a professional appearance and consistency among the staff members.

In a uniform room, uniforms are typically organized by job position and size, making it easier for employees to find and retrieve their specific uniforms. The room may also contain amenities such as mirrors, changing areas, and lockers for staff members to store their personal belongings while on duty.

Uniform rooms are usually managed by a uniform coordinator or supervisor who oversees the distribution, maintenance, and inventory of uniforms. They ensure that an adequate supply of uniforms is available and handle the laundry and cleaning process to keep the uniforms in good condition.

Overall, a uniform room plays a vital role in ensuring that hotel staff members are well-presented, reflecting the hotel's brand image and providing a professional and cohesive appearance to guests.

The issuing and exchange of uniforms in hotels typically follows a standardized process to ensure that employees have the appropriate attire and maintain a professional appearance. Here's an overview of how the issuing and exchange of uniforms in hotels may typically occur:

1. **Initial Uniform Issuance** - When a new employee is hired, they are usually required to visit the uniform room or designated area to be fitted for their uniforms. The employee provides information about their size, role, and any specific uniform requirements. The uniform coordinator or supervisor assists in selecting the appropriate sizes and styles.

2. **Uniform Assignment** - Once the employee's uniforms are selected, they are assigned a set of uniforms for their specific position. This may include items such as shirts, pants/skirts, jackets, aprons, name tags, and other accessories as required by their role.

3. **Documentation and Tracking** - The uniform coordinator maintains a record of the uniforms issued to each employee. This helps in tracking the inventory and ensuring that employees return the uniforms when necessary.

4. **Uniform Care and Maintenance** - Employees are generally responsible for maintaining the cleanliness and proper care of their uniforms. They may be provided with guidelines on how to launder or dry clean the uniforms, or the hotel may have an in-house laundry service. Uniforms may need to be professionally cleaned or laundered at regular intervals to ensure they remain presentable.

5. **Uniform Exchange** - If an employee's uniform becomes damaged, worn-out, or no longer fits, they can request an exchange. The employee informs the uniform coordinator or supervisor about the issue, and arrangements are made to provide a replacement uniform.

6. **Returning Uniforms** - When an employee leaves their position or the hotel, they are usually required to return their uniforms. This helps maintain inventory control and ensures that uniforms are available for new hires or replacements.

7. **Uniform Room Operations** - The uniform room or designated area is managed by the uniform coordinator or supervisor. They oversee the inventory, maintenance, and organization of the uniforms. They may also handle the laundering, repairs, or alterations of uniforms as needed.

It's important for hotels to establish clear guidelines and procedures for issuing and exchanging uniforms to maintain a consistent and professional appearance among their staff members.

The selection and designing of hotel uniforms involve careful consideration of various factors, including the hotel's brand image, the staff's job roles and responsibilities, comfort, functionality, and style. Here's a general overview of the process:

1. **Establish Brand Identity** - The first step is to understand the hotel's brand identity and image. This includes considering the hotel's overall theme, style, and target market. The uniforms should align with the hotel's brand and create a cohesive and professional look.

2. **Identify Job Roles** - Determine the different job roles within the hotel, such as front desk staff, housekeeping, bellmen, concierge, restaurant servers, and spa personnel. Each role may have specific uniform requirements based on their responsibilities and interactions with guests.

3. **Functional Considerations** - Assess the functional requirements of each job role. Consider factors like ease of movement, durability, and practicality. For example, housekeeping staff may require uniforms with pockets for carrying keys and supplies, while front desk staff may need uniforms with easy access to name tags and pens.

4. **Employee Input** - It's beneficial to involve employees in the uniform selection process. Seek their input and feedback regarding comfort, fit, and any specific concerns they may have. This can help ensure that the uniforms are well-received by the staff and contribute to their job satisfaction.

5. **Fabric and Material Selection** - Choose fabrics that are comfortable, durable, and appropriate for the work environment. Consider factors like breathability, wrinkle resistance, and ease of maintenance. Different job roles may require different fabrics and materials, such as moisture-wicking fabrics for restaurant staff or stain-resistant materials for housekeeping.

6. **Style and Design** - Work with a professional uniform designer or consultant to create a design that reflects the hotel's brand and desired image. Consider elements such as colour schemes, patterns, silhouettes, and accessories like ties, scarves, or aprons. The design should be visually appealing, modern, and in line with current fashion trends while remaining consistent with the hotel's brand.

7. **Sample Production and Testing** - Once the design is finalized, create sample uniforms for testing and feedback. Allow employees to try them on and provide input on fit, comfort, and any necessary adjustments. Conduct thorough testing to ensure that the uniforms meet functional requirements and maintain their appearance after cleaning.

8. **Implementation and Rollout** - After finalizing the designs and addressing any necessary changes, proceed with the production and implementation of the uniforms. Establish a timeline for distributing the uniforms to staff members, ensuring proper fittings, and providing guidelines for care and maintenance.

Regularly review and evaluate the uniforms to assess their effectiveness, address any issues or concerns, and make improvements if necessary. The goal is to create uniforms that not only reflect the hotel's brand image but also enhance employee satisfaction and contribute to a positive guest experience.

There are several types of hotel uniforms designed to suit the specific needs and job roles within the hospitality industry. Here are some common types of hotel uniforms:

1. **Front Desk/Reception Uniforms** - These uniforms are typically worn by front desk staff and include elements such as tailored suits, blazers, dress shirts, blouses, ties, scarves, and name tags. The goal is to project professionalism and create a welcoming first impression for guests.

2. **Housekeeping Uniforms** - Housekeeping staff uniforms prioritize functionality and comfort. They often include items such as tunics, smocks, or dresses for women, and shirts with pants or skirts for men. Aprons, name badges, comfortable shoes, and cleaning gloves are also commonly included.

3. **Restaurant and Banquet Uniforms** - Restaurant and banquet staff uniforms vary based on the style and ambiance of the establishment. They can range from formal attire like tailored suits, dresses, and ties for fine dining settings, to more casual outfits for casual dining or themed restaurants. Accessories such as aprons, vests, bow ties, and name tags may be included.

4. **Bartender and Barista Uniforms** - These uniforms are designed for bartenders and baristas and may include elements such as bartender shirts, waistcoats, aprons, and caps. Comfortable and breathable fabrics are often chosen to accommodate the fast-paced nature of their work.

5. **Concierge Uniforms** - Concierge uniforms typically feature a more formal and distinguished appearance to reflect their role as ambassadors of the hotel. This may include items such as tailored suits, blazers, dress shirts, ties, and distinctive accessories like hats or gloves.

6. **Spa and Wellness Uniforms** - Staff working in spas or wellness centers often wear uniforms that convey relaxation and tranquillity . These may include comfortable robes, tunics, or spa dresses, along with appropriate footwear like slippers.

7. **Security Uniforms** - Security personnel require uniforms that are easily identifiable and convey a sense of authority. These uniforms often consist of blazers, shirts, trousers, ties, or badges, along with accessories like hats or caps.

It's important to note that the specific uniform types and designs can vary based on the hotel's brand, theme, and individual preferences. Uniforms should always be comfortable, well-fitted, and reflect the desired image of the hotel while addressing the functional requirements of the job roles within the establishment.

The layout of a uniform room in a hotel may vary depending on the size of the hotel, the number of staff members, and the available space. However, here are some general considerations for designing the layout of a uniform room in a hotel:

1. **Size and Location** - Choose a room that is adequately sized to accommodate the storage and organization of the uniforms. Ideally, it should be easily accessible to the staff members but separate from guest areas. Consider locating it near employee entrances or locker rooms for convenience.

2. **Shelving and Racks** - Install sturdy shelving units and clothing racks to store and organize the uniforms. Utilize adjustable shelves to accommodate different sizes and types of uniforms. Group uniforms by job roles or departments to make it easier for staff members to find their specific uniforms.

3. **Hanging Space** - Provide ample hanging space for uniforms that need to be stored on hangers, such as jackets, blouses, or dresses. Use garment racks or hanging rods to ensure that the uniforms are kept wrinkle-free and easily accessible.

4. **Storage Bins or Drawers** - Use storage bins or drawers to store smaller items like accessories, name tags, or extra buttons. Label these bins or drawers for easy identification and quick access.

5. **Mirrors and Changing Areas -** Include full-length mirrors in the uniform room to allow staff members to check their appearance and ensure proper uniform fit. Designate a small area within the room for staff members to change into their uniforms if needed.

6. **Lockers or Personal Storage** - Provide lockers or designated areas for staff members to store their personal belongings securely while on duty. This helps maintain a clutter-free uniform room and ensures the safety of personal items.

7. **Lighting and Ventilation** - Ensure the uniform room is well-lit with sufficient lighting to allow staff members to see the details of their uniforms. Adequate ventilation is also important to prevent odors and maintain a fresh environment.

8. **Laundry and Cleaning Area** - If possible, designate a separate area within the uniform room or adjacent to it for laundry and cleaning activities. This allows for efficient handling of dirty uniforms, sorting, and organizing of clean uniforms, and proper maintenance of laundry equipment.

9. **Inventory Control System** - Implement an inventory control system to track the issuance, return, and maintenance of uniforms. This can be done through manual record-keeping or by utilizing a computerized system or software specifically designed for uniform management.

Remember to consider safety, accessibility, and efficiency when designing the layout of a uniform room in a hotel. Regularly assess the layout to ensure it meets the evolving needs of the hotel and its staff members.

The recycling of discarded linen in hotels is an environmentally responsible practice that helps reduce waste and promote sustainability. Here are some common methods and considerations for recycling discarded linen:

1. **Sorting and Separation** - Establish a system for properly sorting and separating discarded linen based on their condition and material type. This can include differentiating between clean and soiled linen, as well as segregating items made of different fabrics like cotton, polyester, or blends.

2. **Laundering and Reuse** - Linen that is still in good condition and meets hygiene standards can be laundered and reused within the hotel. Implement procedures to ensure that only linens in good condition are processed for reuse, while any damaged or excessively worn items are set aside for recycling or disposal.

3. **Repurposing** - Consider repurposing discarded linen that cannot be reused as intended. For example, old towels or sheets can be cut into smaller pieces and used as cleaning rags or polishing cloths. This extends the useful life of the linen and reduces the need for single-use items.

4. **Donation** - Establish relationships with local charitable organizations, shelters, or community centers that may have a need for donated linen. Items that are still in usable condition but no longer meet the hotel's standards can be donated to these organizations to benefit those in need.

5. **Recycling Programs** - Explore partnerships with textile recycling companies or facilities that specialize in processing and repurposing textile waste. These organizations have the expertise and infrastructure to properly recycle discarded linen into new products or materials, such as insulation, upholstery, or even new fabric.

6. **Communication and Training** - Ensure that hotel staff members are educated about the importance of linen recycling and are trained on proper sorting procedures. Clear signage and designated collection areas can help facilitate the process and encourage staff to participate.

7. **Monitoring and Evaluation** - Regularly assess and monitor the effectiveness of the linen recycling program. Track the amount of linen being recycled, measure cost savings, and gather feedback from staff members to identify areas for improvement.

By implementing a comprehensive linen recycling program, hotels can significantly reduce the environmental impact of their operations and contribute to a more sustainable and responsible approach to linen management.

There are various types of stains that can occur on fabrics, each requiring different techniques for effective removal . Here are some common types of stains and recommended removal techniques:

1. **Food and Beverage Stains** - These stains include common culprits like coffee, tea, wine, sauces, and grease. For fresh stains, blot the excess liquid or gently scrape off any solid residue. Treat the stain by applying a mixture of mild detergent and water, gently rubbing the fabric together, and then rinsing thoroughly. For stubborn stains, pre-treat with a stain remover or use a specialized product designed for that specific type of stain.

2. **Oil and Grease Stains** - Oil-based stains, such as cooking oil, butter, or makeup, can be challenging to remove. Blot the stain to remove any excess oil. Apply a solvent-based stain remover or a small amount of dishwashing liquid directly to the stain, gently work it in, and then rinse thoroughly. Launder the fabric as usual.

3. **Ink Stains** - Ink stains from pens, markers, or printers can be stubborn. Blot the stain with a clean cloth to absorb as much ink as possible. Apply rubbing alcohol or a specialized ink remover to the stain, then blot with a clean cloth. Rinse thoroughly and launder as usual.

4. **Blood Stains** - For fresh blood stains, rinse the fabric with cold water to remove as much blood as possible. Pre-treat the stain with a mixture of cold water and enzyme-based laundry detergent, gently rubbing the fabric together. Launder the item in cold water. For dried blood stains, soak the fabric in a mixture of cold water and enzyme-based detergent before laundering.

5. **Grass Stains** - Grass stains can be challenging due to their green pigmentation. Pre-treat the stain with a mixture of equal parts vinegar and water, or use a laundry pre-wash stain remover. Gently rub the fabric together, then launder as usual.

6. **Mud Stains** - Allow mud to dry completely before attempting to remove it. Once dry, brush off as much mud as possible. Pre-treat the stain with a mixture of water and liquid laundry detergent or use a stain remover. Launder the fabric as usual in the warmest water appropriate for the fabric.

7. **Sweat Stains** - Sweat stains can leave yellow discoloration on fabrics, particularly in areas like underarms. Pre-treat the stain with a mixture of equal parts white vinegar and water, or use a specialized enzyme-based stain remover. Gently rub the fabric together, then launder as usual.

Remember to always check the fabric care label before attempting stain removal, as certain fabrics may require specific instructions or professional cleaning. It's also a good idea to test any stain removal technique on a small, inconspicuous area of the fabric first to ensure it doesn't cause any damage or discoloration.

CHAPTER 7
Inventory Management

Housekeeping inventory management is a critical aspect of hotel operations. It involves the proper planning, organizing, and controlling of the inventory of housekeeping supplies and equipment. Effective inventory management can help ensure that housekeeping staff have the necessary supplies and equipment to perform their duties efficiently and effectively, while minimizing waste and reducing costs.

Here are some key considerations for housekeeping inventory management in hotels:

1. **Establish par levels** - Determine the minimum level of each item that needs to be maintained in stock at all times. This ensures that the housekeeping staff always has the necessary supplies on hand to perform their tasks.

2. **Conduct regular inventory audits** - Regularly auditing inventory can help identify discrepancies between inventory levels and actual usage. This can help prevent overstocking, stockouts, and waste.

3. **Use inventory management software** - Utilizing an inventory management software can help streamline inventory tracking and ordering. This can help prevent stock-outs and ensure that housekeeping staff have the necessary supplies and equipment to perform their duties.

4. **Develop a standard operating procedure (SOP)** - An SOP can help ensure that inventory management processes are standardized and consistent across the hotel. This can help prevent errors and ensure that the inventory management process is efficient and effective.

5. **Train staff** - Train housekeeping staff on proper inventory management practices. This can help prevent waste, ensure that supplies are used effectively, and reduce costs.

By implementing these practices, hotels can ensure that they have an effective housekeeping inventory management system in place, which can help improve operational efficiency, reduce costs, and enhance the guest experience.

Proper management of supplies and equipment is crucial for housekeeping staff to perform their duties effectively and efficiently. Here are some tips for housekeeping staff to manage supplies and equipment:

1. **Follow established protocols** - Housekeeping staff should adhere to the established protocols for inventory management, including par levels, ordering procedures, and storage guidelines.

2. **Monitor inventory levels** - Staff should monitor inventory levels regularly and report any discrepancies or issues to management. This ensures that supplies and equipment are available when needed.

3. **Use supplies and equipment appropriately** - Staff should use supplies and equipment for their intended purpose and follow manufacturer instructions for use and maintenance.

4. **Store supplies and equipment properly** - Supplies and equipment should be stored in a clean and organized manner to prevent damage or loss. Hazardous materials should be stored safely and securely.

5. **Report damaged or faulty equipment** - Staff should report any damaged or faulty equipment to management immediately to ensure timely repair or replacement.

6. **Use supplies efficiently** - Staff should use supplies efficiently to minimize waste and reduce costs. For example, they should use the appropriate amount of cleaning solution or paper products for each task.

7. **Maintain cleanliness** - Staff should maintain a clean and organized workspace to prevent contamination and promote safety.

By following these practices, housekeeping staff can ensure that supplies and equipment are used effectively and efficiently, which can help improve operational efficiency, reduce costs, and enhance the guest experience.

Managing towels and bedding inventory is a critical aspect of housekeeping operations in hotels. Here are some tips for housekeeping staff to manage towels and bedding inventory:

1. **Set par levels** - Determine the minimum number of towels and bedding items that need to be in stock at all times. This ensures that housekeeping staff always has enough supplies to meet guest needs.

2. **Conduct regular inventory audits** - Regularly auditing inventory can help identify discrepancies between inventory levels and actual usage. This can help prevent overstocking or shortages.

3. **Track usage** - Monitor usage patterns and adjust inventory levels accordingly. For example, during peak season, more towels and bedding may be needed.

4. **Use a tracking system** - Use a tracking system to monitor towel and bedding inventory levels, usage, and orders. This can help ensure that supplies are always available and prevent shortages.

5. **Monitor laundry process** - Ensure that the laundry process is efficient and that towels and bedding are laundered appropriately to extend their lifespan.

6. **Rotate inventory** - Rotate the inventory regularly to prevent items from becoming worn-out or damaged. For example, the oldest towels or bedding should be used first.

7. **Train staff** - Train housekeeping staff on proper inventory management practices, including the handling, storage, and laundering of towels and bedding.

By implementing these practices, housekeeping staff can ensure that towels and bedding inventory is managed effectively and efficiently, which can help improve operational efficiency, reduce costs, and enhance the guest experience.

CHAPTER 8
Safety & Security

Safety and security are top priorities for housekeeping operations in hotels, as they involve working in close proximity to guests' personal belongings. Here are some safety and security protocols that should be followed by housekeeping staff in hotels:

1. **Lock guest room doors** - Ensure that guest room doors are locked when entering or exiting, and never prop open doors to prevent unauthorized access.

2. **Wear identification** - Wear visible identification badges to identify themselves as housekeeping staff.

3. **Knock and announce before entering** - Knock and announce themselves before entering guest rooms to ensure guest privacy and safety.

4. **Check the room before cleaning** - Check for any signs of suspicious activity or safety hazards, such as broken glass or spills, before beginning the cleaning process.

5. **Secure guest belongings** - Handle guest belongings with care and respect, and ensure that they are secure at all times. Never remove items from guest rooms or touch personal belongings.

6. **Report any suspicious activity** - Report any suspicious activity or behaviour immediately to hotel management or security personnel.

7. **Follow safe lifting and handling procedures** - Use proper lifting techniques when moving heavy items, such as furniture or bedding, to prevent injury.

8. **Proper use of chemicals** - Follow appropriate safety procedures when using cleaning chemicals, such as wearing protective gloves and masks, and ensure that chemicals are stored safely and labelled correctly.

9. **Training and drills** - Provide housekeeping staff with proper training and conduct regular safety drills to prepare them for emergency situations .

By following these safety and security protocols, housekeeping staff can ensure the safety and privacy of guests and provide a secure environment for both guests and staff.

Housekeeping staff often work alone in guestrooms, making it essential to follow specific safety protocols to ensure their safety. Here are some safety protocols for housekeeping staff working in guestrooms:

1. **Knock and announce before entering** - Always knock on the door and announce themselves before entering a guestroom to prevent any potential safety incidents or privacy concerns.

2. **Keep the door open or use doorstop** - When entering the room, keep the door open or use a doorstop to prevent being locked in or trapped.

3. **Check the room before entering** - Before entering the room, check for any safety hazards such as spilled liquids or trip hazards.

4. **Avoid working alone** - Where possible, work with a colleague or inform other staff members about their location when working alone.

5. **Be alert to suspicious activity** - Be alert to any suspicious activity or behaviour in the guestroom and report it immediately to hotel management or security personnel.

6. **Use PPE** - Use personal protective equipment (PPE) such as gloves, masks, and safety goggles when handling hazardous materials, cleaning chemicals, or contaminated items.

7. **Use proper lifting techniques** - Use proper lifting techniques and equipment when moving heavy objects, such as furniture, to prevent back injuries.

8. **Use the right tools** - Use the appropriate cleaning tools and equipment, such as ladders or step stools, to prevent falls or injuries.

9. **Know emergency protocols** - Familiarize themselves with the hotel's emergency protocols, such as evacuation plans, and know how to contact emergency services in case of an emergency.

By following these safety protocols, housekeeping staff can minimize safety risks and provide a secure environment for themselves and hotel guests.

Public areas in hotels, such as lobbies, restaurants, and hallways, can pose safety risks for guests and staff. Here are some safety protocols for housekeeping staff working in public areas of hotels:

1. **Be aware of surroundings** - Be aware of their surroundings at all times and report any safety hazards, such as wet floors, damaged furniture, or tripping hazards, to hotel management or maintenance staff.

2. **Use caution with equipment** - Use caution when using equipment, such as vacuum cleaners or floor polishers, to avoid accidents or injuries.

3. **Use proper lifting techniques** - Use proper lifting techniques and equipment when moving heavy objects, such as furniture or equipment, to prevent back injuries.

4. **Use proper PPE** - Use personal protective equipment (PPE) such as gloves, masks, and safety goggles when handling hazardous materials, cleaning chemicals, or contaminated items.

5. **Secure storage areas** - Ensure that storage areas for cleaning supplies and equipment are secure and inaccessible to guests to prevent accidents or misuse.

6. **Be mindful of guests** - Be mindful of guest traffic in public areas and avoid working in areas that may be disruptive or unsafe for guests.

7. **Follow electrical safety procedures** - Follow electrical safety procedures when using electrical equipment and avoid using damaged or frayed cords or plugs.

8. **Follow emergency protocols** - Be familiar with the hotel's emergency protocols, such as evacuation plans, and know how to contact emergency services in case of an emergency.

By following these safety protocols, housekeeping staff can minimize safety risks in public areas of hotels and provide a safe environment for both guests and staff.

If a hotel guest is confirmed to be COVID-19 positive, it is crucial for the hotel to act promptly and responsibly to prevent further spread of the virus and ensure the safety of other guests and staff. Here are the steps a hotel should take in such a situation:

1. **Isolate the guest** - If the guest informs the hotel staff about their positive COVID-19 status, or if the hotel becomes aware of it through other means, the guest should be isolated immediately in a designated area or room with proper ventilation.

2. **Notify the authorities** - The hotel should contact the local health authorities and inform them about the positive case. Follow their guidance on how to proceed and any necessary contact tracing measures .

3. **Protect staff** - Hotel staff who had direct contact with the COVID-19 positive guest should be informed immediately. They should be provided with appropriate personal protective equipment (PPE) and guidance on monitoring their health and seeking medical attention if they develop symptoms.

4. **Contact tracing** - The hotel should work with health authorities to identify any guests or staff who may have come into close contact with the positive guest during their stay. Those individuals should be informed of their potential exposure and advised to take appropriate precautions, such as self-monitoring and getting tested.

5. **Deep cleaning and sanitization** - The room where the COVID-19 positive guest stayed should be thoroughly cleaned and disinfected following the guidelines and recommendations of health authorities. Pay special attention to high-touch surfaces like doorknobs, light switches, remote controls, and bathroom fixtures.

6. **Communicate with guests** - It's essential to be transparent and communicate with other guests about the situation without revealing the identity of the COVID-19 positive guest. Inform them of the actions being taken to ensure their safety and the hotel's commitment to maintaining a clean and safe environment.

7. **Temporarily close affected areas** - If necessary, the hotel may consider temporarily closing the affected area or floor to conduct thorough cleaning and sanitization.

8. **Review and update protocols** - The hotel management should review their COVID-19 protocols and update them if necessary to prevent future incidents and improve the response to similar situations.

9. **Assist the guest** - If the COVID-19 positive guest needs medical assistance or transportation to a healthcare facility, the hotel should arrange for appropriate support and follow local health guidelines.

10. **Monitor the situation** - Continue to monitor the health status of staff and guests and be prepared to take additional measures if needed, following the guidance of health authorities.

Response to Pandemic Situation

It's essential for hotels to have a comprehensive COVID-19 response plan in place to handle such situations effectively and protect the health and well-being of everyone involved. Adhering to local health guidelines and maintaining open communication with guests and staff are key factors in managing a COVID-19 positive case in a hotel setting.

High touch point disinfection is a critical aspect of hotel cleaning protocols, especially during the COVID-19 pandemic and other times when hygiene is a top priority. High touch points are surfaces that are frequently touched by multiple people and have the potential to harbor germs and viruses. Proper disinfection of these areas helps reduce the risk of transmission and ensures a safe and healthy environment for guests and staff. Here are some common high touch points in hotels and guidelines for their disinfection:

1. **Reception/Check-in Area:**
    - Disinfect reception desks, counters, and credit card machines regularly.
    - Clean and disinfect pens and styluses used for signing documents.
    - Wipe down key cards or electronic key card readers.

2. **Elevators and Stair Railings:**
    - Disinfect elevator buttons, both inside and outside the elevators, regularly.
    - Clean stair railings frequently, especially in high traffic areas.

3. **Door Handles and Knobs:**
    - Disinfect door handles and knobs of guest room doors, common area doors, and restroom doors.

- Pay special attention to entrance and exit doors, as they are frequently touched by multiple people.

4. **Handrails:**

    - Regularly disinfect handrails on staircases, escalators, and any other locations with handrails.

5. **Light Switches:**

    - Disinfect light switches in guest rooms, hallways, and common areas.

6. **Remote Controls:**

    - Clean and disinfect TV remotes and other electronic devices in guest rooms.

7. **Public Restrooms:**

    - Regularly disinfect toilet handles, flush buttons, faucet handles, soap dispensers, and paper towel dispensers.
    - Provide touchless options for soap dispensers, faucets, and hand dryers when possible.

8. **Gym and Fitness Equipment:**

    - Disinfect gym equipment handles, buttons, and touch screens after each use.
    - Encourage guests to clean equipment before and after use with provided disinfecting wipes.

9. **Dining Areas and Buffets:**

    - Disinfect dining tables, chairs, and high chairs between each use.
    - If using self-service buffet stations, ensure regular cleaning and disinfection of serving utensils and surfaces.

10. **Public Area Furniture:**

    - Regularly clean and disinfect furniture in lobby areas, lounges, and other common spaces.

11. Vending Machines:

- Disinfect vending machine buttons and touch screens regularly.

12. Guestroom Amenities:

- Clean and disinfect in-room amenities such as telephones, alarm clocks, and minibar handles.

It's essential for hotels to establish clear protocols and provide training to housekeeping staff on the proper use of disinfectants and the frequency of disinfection for high touch points. Using EPA-approved disinfectants and following the manufacturer's instructions for their proper use is crucial for effective disinfection. Additionally, maintaining an open line of communication with guests about the hotel's cleaning efforts and commitment to their safety can provide reassurance and build trust.

CHAPTER 9
Communication & Customer Service

Effective communication is essential for housekeeping staff to ensure that guests' needs and expectations are met. Here are some ways housekeeping staff can communicate effectively with guests:

1. **Use a friendly tone** - Greet guests with a friendly tone and smile when entering the room or interacting with them.

2. **Use clear and concise language** - Use clear and concise language when communicating with guests, avoiding jargon or technical terms that may confuse them.

3. **Listen actively** - Listen actively to guests' concerns and needs and respond appropriately.

4. **Be responsive** - Be responsive to guests' requests, providing timely and efficient service.

5. **Provide helpful information** - Provide helpful information to guests about hotel services, amenities, and local attractions.

6. **Respect guest privacy** - Respect guest privacy and avoid entering the room without permission or disturbing them when they are resting.

7. **Be proactive** - Be proactive in identifying and resolving any issues or concerns before they become problems.

8. **Use non-verbal communication** - Use nonverbal communication, such as eye contact and body language, to convey warmth and sincerity.

9. **Speak the guest's language** - If possible, speak the guest's language or provide translation services to ensure effective communication.

By following these communication strategies, housekeeping staff can create a positive guest experience and build trust and rapport with guests. Effective communication can also help prevent misunderstandings and complaints, leading to higher guest satisfaction and loyalty.

Delivering exceptional customer service is essential for housekeeping staff to ensure that guests have a positive experience and feel valued. Here is a tip for housekeeping staff to deliver exceptional customer service:

Pay attention to the small details

Guests often notice and appreciate small details in their room, such as neatly folded towels, freshly made beds, and clean surfaces. Paying attention to these details can make a big difference in the guest experience and help create a positive impression of the hotel.

Here are some specific ways housekeeping staff can pay attention to the small details:

1. **Use high-quality cleaning products** - Use high-quality cleaning products to ensure that surfaces are clean and free of dust and dirt.

2. **Check for and remove any stains or marks** - Check for and remove any stains or marks on surfaces or fabrics, such as carpeting or upholstery.

3. **Make sure bedding is neatly arranged** - Make sure bedding is neatly arranged and free of wrinkles, with pillows fluffed and placed in an orderly manner.

4. **Fold towels and linens neatly** - Fold towels and linens neatly and in a consistent manner, so they look tidy and presentable.

5. **Pay attention to room amenities** - Ensure that room amenities, such as toiletries and coffee supplies, are fully stocked and arranged neatly.

6. **Leave a personal touch** - Leave a personal touch, such as a handwritten note, to show guests that you value their stay and appreciate their business.

By paying attention to the small details, housekeeping staff can create a memorable guest experience and exceed guest expectations.

Soft Touches

Soft touches by housekeeping refer to the extra care and attention to detail that housekeeping staff provide while cleaning guest rooms. These small gestures can make a significant difference in enhancing the guest experience and creating a warm, welcoming environment. Here are some examples of soft touches by housekeeping:

1. **Bed Arrangement** - Housekeeping staff may arrange the pillows neatly on the bed, add decorative touches like folded towel swans, or place a decorative throw blanket to create an inviting atmosphere.

2. **Linen Folding** - Folding towels and bathrobes in a creative or elegant manner can add a thoughtful touch to the bathroom and make guests feel special.

3. **Personalized Notes** - Leaving a handwritten thank-you note or a personalized message for the guest can show appreciation and make the guest feel valued.

4. **Organized Amenities** - Ensuring that all amenities, such as toiletries and coffee supplies, are neatly arranged and fully stocked can make guests feel well-cared for.

5. **Removing Clutter** - Housekeeping may tidy up any personal items left by the guest, such as shoes or clothes, and organize them in a neat manner.

6. **Artful Arrangement** - Rearranging magazines or books on the bedside table or arranging the guest's belongings in a visually appealing way can add a touch of elegance to the room.

7. **Temperature and Lighting** - Adjusting the room temperature to a comfortable level and setting the lighting to create a cozy ambiance can make guests feel at ease.

8. **Fresh Flowers** - Some hotels may place a small vase of fresh flowers in the room to add a touch of nature and freshness.

9. **In-Room Entertainment** - Housekeeping may set up the television or music system with a soothing channel or playlist to welcome guests to a relaxing environment.

10. **Curtains and Views** - Ensuring that curtains or blinds are drawn correctly to showcase a beautiful view or create a serene atmosphere can add to the overall experience.

11. **Attentive Cleaning** - Paying attention to detail while cleaning, such as removing dust from all surfaces, ensuring spotless mirrors, and tidying up corners, shows the commitment to maintaining a clean and well-maintained room.

These soft touches by housekeeping not only create a positive impression but also contribute to the overall guest satisfaction and comfort during their stay. They demonstrate the hotel's dedication to providing a personalized and memorable experience for each guest.

Crafting exquisite tea experiences for modern connoisseurs

The Inspiration

For over a century The Hillcart Tales has proudly upheld the tradition of crafting blends of exceptional and rare teas each reflecting its own distinctive origin. Our story commenced amidst the rolling hills, tea plantations and the awe inspiring presence of Kanchenjunga captivating our founder, Ashutosh Ghosh who developed a passion for the artistry of tea.

A Legacy of Rare Blends

At The Hillcart Tales we honour the vision of our founder by choosing and combining teas that capture the essence of their origins. Every cup is an adventure—a voyage through time, historical narratives and the breathtaking scenery that has been a source of inspiration for generations. Let The Hillcart Tales be your guide to the world of tea, where tradition meets the modern connoisseur. Experience the exquisite flavours and enduring legacy of fine blended rare teas.

Why savour a cup of tea from The Hillcart Tales?

Precise Sourcing

We selectively handpick our shoots making sure that only the first few tender leaves and the iconic still-curled bud reaches our bouquet of offerings.

Master Blending

Our master blenders weave their magic delving into the finest details, building structure, form and meaning into every sip to be savoured reminiscing our age-old traditions.

Bespoke Packaging

We believe that the presentation of our teas should be as exquisite as the teas themselves. To preserve the aromatic and flavour integrity of our brew, the tea leaves are enclosed in individually handcrafted muslin bags which are packaged into coaster pods adorned with handpicked quotes. Our sustainable boxes can be upcycled into various household décor accessories, adding value to your purchase.

Rare Flavours Crafted

Above all, our commitment is to craft exquisite and rare flavours that transport you to the heart of tea culture. Every sip is an invitation to experience centuries of tea mastery.

CHAPTER 10
Environment Sustainability

Reducing a hotel's environmental impact is essential to ensure sustainable operations and promote responsible tourism. Here are some ways housekeeping staff can reduce a hotel's environmental impact:

1. **Use eco-friendly cleaning products** - Switch to eco-friendly cleaning products that are biodegradable, non-toxic, and use less water.

2. **Use energy-efficient equipment** - Use energy-efficient cleaning equipment such as vacuum cleaners and washing machines, which can save energy and reduce water consumption.

3. **Reduce water consumption** - Implement water-saving practices, such as using low-flow showerheads, faucets, and toilets, and encourage guests to reuse towels and linens.

4. **Proper waste management** - Proper waste management by segregating recyclable and non-recyclable materials and disposal of hazardous waste according to regulations.

5. **Use natural lighting** - Use natural lighting to minimize energy consumption and promote a healthier environment.

6. **Monitor temperature settings** - Monitor and adjust temperature settings in guest rooms and public areas to reduce energy consumption and promote energy efficiency.

7. **Encourage sustainable practices** - Encourage guests to adopt sustainable practices such as using reusable water bottles, bags and avoiding disposable plastics.

8. **Reuse materials** - Reuse and repurpose materials whenever possible, such as using old linens as cleaning rags, to reduce waste and promote resource efficiency.

By implementing these practices, housekeeping staff can significantly reduce a hotel's environmental impact and promote sustainability. They can also educate guests on sustainable practices, thereby creating awareness and encouraging more responsible travel behavior.

Energy-saving practices are essential for housekeeping staff to reduce a hotel's carbon footprint and promote sustainable operations. Here are some ways housekeeping staff can implement energy-saving practices:

1. **Turn off lights and electronic devices** - Encourage staff to turn off lights and electronic devices such as TVs, radios, and air conditioning units when not in use in guest rooms and public areas.

2. **Use energy-efficient lighting** - Use energy-efficient light bulbs such as LED, CFL, and T5 lighting that consume less energy and last longer than traditional bulbs.

3. **Optimize laundry operations** - Optimize laundry operations such as adjusting machine settings and load sizes, and washing in cold water, to reduce energy consumption and prolong equipment life.

4. **Proper maintenance** - Perform proper maintenance of equipment such as HVAC systems, refrigeration units, and laundry machines, to ensure that they run efficiently and consume less energy.

5. **Adjust thermostat settings** - Adjust thermostat settings in guest rooms and public areas to reduce energy consumption and promote energy efficiency.

6. **Use natural lighting** - Use natural lighting whenever possible to minimize the use of artificial light, and use window treatments such as blinds and shades to control light and heat.

7. **Insulate windows and doors** - Insulate windows and doors to prevent air leaks, which can help to reduce energy consumption and improve thermal comfort.

By implementing these energy-saving practices, housekeeping staff can significantly reduce a hotel's energy consumption, save on operational costs, and promote sustainability. They can also educate guests on energy-saving practices, thereby creating awareness and encouraging more responsible travel behavior.

KH KIMIRICA HUNTER®

A Luxurious and Sustainable Future: Kimirica Hunter International's Vision for Hotel Amenities.

Kimirica was started by Rajat Jain & Mohit Jain in 2013 with a vision to organize the Hospitality Personal Care industry in India. At a point when almost 95% toiletries and amenities were imported from China, this duo managed to bring most groups on-board for their supplies.

Today Hotel Chains like Marriott, Hyatt, Accor, The Leela, and many more are trusting Kimirica as their preferred partner. Kimirica Ventures is now a group of companies with a diverse portfolio of ventures catering to industries including personal care, hospitality and IT products to over 40 countries in the world.

In the realm of luxury hospitality, where every detail counts, Kimirica Hunter International, an Indore based start-up stands tall as India's largest manufacturer of hotel amenities. A dynamic Indo-Canadian joint venture, Kimirica embodies a commitment to excellence, luxury, and sustainability. Our story is one of passion, purpose, and a relentless pursuit of creating memorable guest experiences.

Luxury Amenities: At Kimirica, we offer a diverse range of meticulously curated brands tailored to meet the unique needs of hotels and resorts.

We take immense pride in offering a portfolio that includes luxury brands like Ignis, Earth, Five Elements, French Note, Herbalist, The Indian Apothecary, as well as internationally licensed brands like Pharmacopia, Portico, June Jacobs and others. Our 100% vegan bath and body care essentials, available in dispensers and miniatures, epitomize luxury in a compact form.

Our exclusive guest room dry accessories range is ideal for the most luxurious hotels, whilst being affordable for economic properties. Our creative offerings include sustainable, eco-friendly options like cornstarch amenities, brown paper pouches, and bamboo amenities, bringing eco-consciousness and sophistication to guest rooms.

Recognizing the importance of personalization and customization in defining the luxurious experience, we craft custom exclusive fragrances, custom labels, and packaging for hotels, with options for bottles, dispensers, and tubes.

Our Green Overture prioritizes ecological stewardship, we craft with the wisdom of efficiency, using "Cold-Process" techniques, and prudent water use, ensuring our products are biodegradable and safe for groundwater.

At Kimirica, we source renewable plant materials and certified herbal ingredients, focusing on safety, quality, and eco-packaging. Rigorous testing ensconced every product, from concept to market debut. The majority of bottled products are made from 100% recyclable PET material.

Creating Impact Since a Decade:-

- KH's story is a true embodiment of the "Made in India" success narrative.
- Esteemed Clients include Marriott, Hilton, Hyatt, The Leela, IHCL, Accor, and an array of independent luxury hotels.
- Promoting Sustainable Products ensuring a greener future.
- We are proud to have achieved a workforce of 50% women, demonstrating our commitment to diversity and inclusion.
- KH proudly wears the badge of being the first 100 percent vegan, paraben-free and fairtrade certified company in hospitality supplies in India over the past decade.

CHAPTER 11
Brand Standards

Housekeeping brand standards refer to the set of guidelines and criteria that define the expected level of cleanliness, maintenance, and overall appearance for a particular brand or hotel chain. These standards ensure consistency and quality across different properties and help create a positive and uniform guest experience.

Here are some common elements found in housekeeping brand standards:

1. **Cleanliness** - This includes specific instructions on how to clean different areas of a hotel room, such as beds, bathrooms, floors, and surfaces. It outlines the frequency of cleaning tasks, the use of appropriate cleaning products, and the importance of maintaining a hygienic environment.

2. **Maintenance** - Brand standards typically cover the regular inspection and maintenance of equipment, fixtures, and amenities to ensure they are in good working condition. This includes checking and repairing items like air conditioning, heating systems, plumbing, and electrical fixtures.

3. **Appearance** - Brand standards often provide guidelines on the visual presentation of the hotel room, common areas, and public spaces. This includes instructions on arranging furniture, organizing items, and maintaining a visually appealing and welcoming atmosphere.

4. **Safety and Security** - Housekeeping brand standards also address safety and security protocols. This may include guidelines on handling hazardous materials, storing cleaning supplies properly, reporting maintenance issues promptly, and ensuring guest safety through measures like proper lighting and well-maintained locks.

5. **Training and Staffing** - Standards may outline the training requirements for housekeeping staff, including procedures for onboarding, ongoing training, and certification programs. It may also specify staff-to-room ratios to ensure adequate coverage for cleaning and maintenance tasks.

6. **Environmental Sustainability** - With increasing emphasis on sustainability, many brand standards now include guidelines for eco-friendly practices. This may involve promoting energy efficiency, waste reduction and recycling, the use of environmentally friendly cleaning products, and encouraging guests to participate in sustainable practices.

7. **Quality Assurance** - Many hotel chains have quality assurance programs to monitor and evaluate housekeeping performance. This may involve regular inspections, audits, or mystery shopper programs to ensure compliance with brand standards and identify areas for improvement.

It's important to note that specific housekeeping brand standards can vary between hotel chains and individual brands within the same chain. Each brand may have its own unique requirements and expectations.

CHAPTER 12
Housekeeping Pantry & Trolley Management

Pantry and trolley setup in housekeeping refers to the organization and arrangement of supplies, equipment, and tools on a housekeeping trolley or in a pantry area. These setups are essential for efficient and effective cleaning operations. Here are some considerations for pantry and trolley setup in housekeeping:

1. **Pantry Setup:**

- **Location** - The pantry should be centrally located and easily accessible to housekeeping staff.

- **Storage** - Proper storage shelves, cabinets, or racks should be available to store cleaning supplies, amenities, linens, and other housekeeping materials.

- **Labelling** - Clearly label and categorize different items to ensure easy identification and retrieval.

- **Stock Management** - Implement a system to track inventory levels and restock items as needed.

- **Safety Measures** - Follow safety guidelines for storing hazardous materials and ensure proper ventilation, lighting, and fire safety measures are in place.

2. **Housekeeping Trolley Setup**:

- **Equipment**: The trolley should be equipped with essential tools and equipment such as vacuum cleaners, brooms, mops, dusters, cleaning cloths, trash bags, and gloves.

- **Segregation**: Organize items on the trolley in a logical and practical manner. For example, place cleaning chemicals and supplies in one section, tools in another, and fresh linens or amenities in a separate area.

- **Accessibility**: Arrange frequently used items within easy reach to minimize the need for excessive bending or stretching.

- **Safety Considerations**: Ensure that potentially hazardous items, such as chemicals, are securely stored and won't spill or cause accidents during movement.

- **Cleanliness**: Regularly clean and sanitize the trolley to maintain hygiene standards.

3. **Organization and Restocking:**

- **Regular Maintenance**: Inspect and organize the pantry and trolley on a regular basis, removing any expired or damaged items and replacing them as necessary.

- **Stock Replenishment**: Keep track of inventory levels and restock supplies to avoid running out during cleaning tasks.

- **Standardized Setup**: Establish a consistent layout and organization system for the pantry and trolley across all housekeeping staff, making it easier for everyone to locate and use items efficiently.

Overall, a well-organized pantry and properly set up housekeeping trolley contribute to a smoother workflow, reduce time wastage, and ensure that housekeeping staff have easy access to the necessary tools and supplies to perform their duties effectively.

CHAPTER 13
Preventive maintenance program

In the context of hotels, preventive maintenance plays a crucial role in ensuring the smooth operation of various systems, equipment, and facilities within the property. Here are some key areas of focus for preventive maintenance in hotels:

1. **Guest Rooms:**

- **HVAC Systems** - Regularly inspect and service heating, ventilation, and air conditioning systems to maintain optimal performance and guest comfort.

- **Plumbing** - Check for leaks, repair or replace faucets, showerheads, toilets, and ensure proper water pressure.

- **Electrical** - Inspect and maintain electrical outlets, switches, lighting fixtures, and ensure safe wiring practices.

- **Doors, Locks, and Safety Features** - Regularly check and maintain door locks, hinges, safety latches, smoke detectors, and fire alarms.

2. **Common Areas:**

- **Elevators** - Perform regular inspections, lubrication, and maintenance of elevator systems to ensure safety and smooth operation.

- **Lighting** - Inspect and replace bulbs, repair faulty switches, and maintain adequate lighting in hallways, lobbies, stairwells, and other public areas.

- **Flooring** - Regularly clean, repair, and replace carpets, tiles, or other flooring materials to maintain a clean and safe environment.

3. **Food and Beverage Facilities:**

- **Kitchen Equipment** - Conduct regular maintenance and cleaning of kitchen appliances, such as ovens, refrigerators, dishwashers, and ventilation systems.

- **Plumbing and Drainage** - Inspect and clean drains, grease traps, and pipes to prevent blockages and ensure proper water flow.

- **Fire Safety** - Maintain and test fire suppression systems, fire extinguishers, and kitchen hood ventilation to comply with safety regulations.

4. **Mechanical and Electrical Systems:**

- **Generators** - Regularly service and test backup generators to ensure they are operational during power outages.

- **Water Supply and Treatment** - Inspect and maintain water pumps, water tanks, filtration systems, and water treatment facilities to ensure water quality and availability.

- **Electrical Distribution** - Inspect electrical panels, transformers, switchboards, and ensure proper grounding and electrical safety measures.

5. **Swimming Pools and Spas:**

- **Water Quality** - Regularly test and treat pool water to maintain proper chemical balance and prevent the growth of bacteria or algae.

- **Pool Equipment** - Inspect and service pool pumps, filters, heaters, and other equipment to ensure efficient operation and guest safety.

6. **Safety and Security:**

- **CCTV and Access Control Systems** - Regularly test and maintain surveillance cameras, access control systems, and ensure proper functioning.

- **Fire Protection** - Inspect and test fire alarm systems, sprinklers, emergency lighting, and other fire safety equipment.

- **Emergency Exits** - Ensure emergency exits are unobstructed, well-marked, and in good working condition.

It's important for hotels to establish a preventive maintenance schedule, document maintenance activities, track equipment warranties, and collaborate with qualified maintenance contractors or technicians to ensure proper and timely servicing of hotel facilities. This helps reduce downtime, maintain guest satisfaction, and prolong the lifespan of assets.

Below is a checklist illustration of how a preventive maintenance checklist appears:

PPM ROOM CHECKLIST				
PPM CHECKLIST #ROOM:			Inspection Date	
COMPLETED BY: Period01 COMPLETED BY: Period02				
	No.	Description	Status	Remarks
ELECTRICAL	1	Check all Switches are in operational		
	2	Check standing and bedside lamps		
	3	Check Lamp shade clean		
	4	Check for fused bulbs		
	5	Check Mirror lights &Shaver socket power		
	6	Check all Power sockets are in operation		
	7	Check Hairdryer is in operation		
	8	Living room Minibar fridge Temp(°C)		
	9	Electrical DB in Room Checked		
	10	Check Safe box battery &operation		
	11	Check Emergency light operation		
HVAC	12	Note Noise Level in room in decibels(dB).		
	13	Visually inspect Motorized valve(open18°C/close28°C)		
	14	Check air filter		
	15	Check condensate drain		
	16	Check Chilled water strainer		
	17	Check TFA supply Temp(°C)		
	18	Motors valve Mechanical testing		
	19	Check the Exhaust working properly		

Section	No.	Description		
	20	Record Temp at Ac vent grill(°C)		
	21	Record Room Temperature(°C)		
	22	Check AC Motor is normal operation		
	23	Check and make sure all valve in proper position		
AV	24	Check All TV Channels working		
	25	Test Remote control function		
	26	Telephone line is in operation		
	27	Bathroom speaker functional		
	28	Door Bell		
	29	PA speaker		
	30	Check the Cable Management is in proper		
Section	**No.**	**Description**		
PLUMBING	31	Check the Toilet WC Flush Valve		
	32	Check the WC seat cover any crack, stain& hinges loose		
	33	Check/repair the Toilet seal for evidence of leaks		
	34	Check the Toilet Tissue holder		
	35	Check the Aerator		
	36	Check sink bottle trap		
	37	Check all mixing valve (Hot & Cold)		
	38	Check and Record the Hot water Temp.(°C)		
	39	Check and Record the Cold water Temp.(°C)		
	40	Check the shower enclosure tracks & door		
	41	Check the shower enclosure bumpers & door handle		
	42	Check the floor drain		
	43	Check soap dish, grab bars & towel bars		
	44	Shaver socket and power point		
	45	Check floor & wall tiles		
	46	Check silicon quality &workmanship		

rowspan	47	Check room number plate for any damage			
	48	Check Main door lock battery if necessary			
	49	Check for door hinge if necessary			
	50	Check the Door Night Latch is functional			
	51	Check Fire Exit plan clearly visible			
	52	Check the Peep Hole visibility			
	53	Check drawer handle & knobs			
	54	Check polish touch up stain &scratches on all furniture			
	55	Check window blinds			
	56	Check Blue TV console glass for finish			
	57	Check all sheer curtain blind smooth in operation			
	58	Check writing table and chair if necessary			
	59	Check the floor carpet if necessary			
	60	Check Bedroom headboard			
	61	Bathroom sliding door			
CIVIL	62	Check wallpaper as necessary			
	63	Check Ceiling paint if necessary			

Technician name:

Duty engineer:

CHAPTER 14
Pest Controlling

Pest control is crucial in hotels to maintain a clean and hygienic environment for guests. Infestations of pests such as bed bugs, cockroaches, rodents, and flies can lead to negative guest experiences, damage to reputation, and potential legal issues. Here are some essential steps and considerations for implementing effective pest control in hotels:

1. **Regular Inspections** - Conduct routine inspections of rooms, common areas, and back-of-house areas to identify any signs of pest activity. Trained professionals should inspect furniture, mattresses, linens, carpets, and other potential hiding spots.

2. **Develop a Pest Control Plan** - Work with a professional pest control company to develop a comprehensive plan tailored to your hotel's specific needs. This plan should include details about prevention, monitoring, treatment procedures, and regular follow-ups.

3. **Training and Education** - Train staff members, especially housekeeping and maintenance personnel, on how to identify signs of pests and report them promptly. They should be aware of best practices for prevention, such as proper waste disposal, food storage, and cleaning procedures.

4. **Integrated Pest Management (IPM)** - Implement an Integrated Pest Management approach, which focuses on long-term prevention and uses a combination of non-chemical and chemical control methods. This may include sealing cracks and crevices, installing door sweeps, maintaining proper sanitation, and targeted pesticide application if necessary.

5. **Bed Bug Prevention** - Bed bugs are a significant concern in hotels. Consider using mattress encasements, regularly inspecting rooms, and implementing

preventive measures like steam cleaning, vacuuming, and heat treatments for infested areas.

6. **Exterior Pest Control -** Pay attention to the exterior of your hotel as well. Proper landscaping, regular garbage removal, and pest-proofing measures can help prevent pests from entering the building.

7. **Record-Keeping -** Maintain detailed records of pest control activities, including inspections, treatments, and any corrective measures taken. These records can be useful for tracking patterns, identifying areas that require additional attention, and demonstrating compliance with regulatory requirements.

8. **Guest Communication** - Provide educational materials or signage in guest rooms, informing them about your pest control efforts and what they can do to prevent issues . Encourage guests to report any pest sightings promptly.

9. **Ongoing Monitoring and Evaluation** - Regularly monitor the effectiveness of your pest control measures through inspections and feedback from staff and guests. Make adjustments to your plan as needed to address any emerging issues or changing circumstances.

Remember, it is essential to work with professional pest control experts who are experienced in handling the unique challenges of the hospitality industry. Compliance with local regulations and health standards is crucial to ensure a safe and pest-free environment for guests and employees.

Fumigation is a pest control method that involves the use of gaseous pesticides to eliminate pests in a specific area. While fumigation can be an effective approach for certain pest infestations, it is generally not recommended for use in occupied hotel rooms due to potential health and safety concerns for guests and staff. The use of fumigation in hotels is typically reserved for specific situations and areas where occupants can be completely evacuated, and strict safety protocols are followed.

If you are facing a severe pest infestation in a hotel, it is crucial to consult with a professional pest control company experienced in hotel environments. They will assess the situation and recommend the most appropriate pest control methods based on the specific pest species, extent of the infestation, and the safety of occupants.

Alternative pest control methods that are commonly used in occupied hotel rooms include:

1. **Integrated Pest Management (IPM)** - This approach combines various pest control techniques, such as physical barriers, traps, targeted pesticide application, and preventive measures, to manage pests effectively with minimal impact on guests and the environment.

2. **Heat Treatments** - High-temperature treatments, such as heat chambers or steam treatments, can be effective for eliminating bed bugs, as they are sensitive to heat. These methods can be used in specific areas without requiring the complete evacuation of the hotel.

3. **Chemical Treatments** - Targeted pesticide applications using approved and safe insecticides can be performed in affected areas. It is essential to work with licensed professionals who follow industry regulations and guidelines for pesticide use.

4. **Ongoing Monitoring and Prevention** - Regular inspections and monitoring of hotel rooms and common areas can help identify and address pest issues at an early stage. Implement preventive measures such as sealing entry points, proper waste management, and regular cleaning protocols.

Remember, the safety and well-being of hotel guests and staff should always be a top priority. Consult with pest control professionals to determine the most appropriate and safe methods for dealing with pests in your hotel.

Fumigation

Fumigation methods in hotels are typically reserved for situations where the entire property or specific areas can be completely sealed off and evacuated, ensuring the safety of guests and staff. Fumigation involves the use of gaseous pesticides, known as fumigants, to eradicate pests throughout a given space. Here are the general steps involved in fumigation in a hotel setting:

1. **Pest Assessment -** Identify the specific pest problem and assess the extent of the infestation. This step helps determine whether fumigation is the most suitable method and which areas require treatment.

2. **Consultation with Professionals** - Engage a licensed and experienced pest control company that specializes in fumigation services. They will evaluate the situation, develop a comprehensive fumigation plan, and provide guidance on necessary preparations and safety measures.

3. **Guest and Staff Evacuation** - Before fumigation begins, guests and staff must be relocated to a safe location away from the treated areas. Proper communication and coordination with guests are essential to minimize inconvenience.

4. **Seal Off the Area** - The fumigation area must be sealed off to contain the fumigant and prevent its dispersion into other parts of the hotel. This involves sealing doors, windows, vents, and any other openings that could allow the gas to escape.

5. **Fumigation Process** - The selected fumigant is released into the sealed space in gas form. The fumigant penetrates into cracks, crevices, and other hiding places to eliminate pests.

6. **Exposure Period** - The fumigant needs to stay in the treated area for a specific period to ensure effective pest elimination. This time-frame depends on the fumigant used, pest species, and other factors determined by the pest control professionals.

7. **Aeration and Ventilation** - After the exposure period, the fumigant must be carefully removed from the treated space. The area is ventilated to allow fresh air to replace the fumigant gas and reduce its concentration to safe levels.

8. **Verification and Safety Checks** - Pest control professionals conduct thorough inspections and measurements to ensure that the treated areas are safe for re-entry. They use specialized equipment to verify that fumigant residues are below acceptable levels.

9. **Clean-up and Preparation for Guests** - Once the area is deemed safe, the space is thoroughly cleaned, and any remaining traces of the fumigant are removed. The hotel can then prepare for guests to return to the treated areas.

It is crucial to note that fumigation in hotels is a complex process that requires expertise and strict adherence to safety protocols. Working with experienced pest control professionals is vital to ensure the effective and safe implementation of fumigation methods

Fogging is a pest control method that involves the use of specialized equipment to disperse a fine mist or fog of insecticides or disinfectants throughout a designated area. In the context of hotels, fogging is commonly employed for insect control, sanitization, and odour control in certain circumstances. Here's an overview of fogging in hotels:

1. **Pest Assessment** - Identify the specific pest problem or the need for sanitization or odour control. Assess the areas that require fogging and determine the appropriate fogging solution to address the issue.

2. **Consultation with Professionals** - Engage a professional pest control company or a specialized fogging service provider. They will evaluate the situation, recommend suitable fogging products, and advise on safety measures and preparations.

3. **Preparations** - Before fogging, certain preparations may be necessary. These can include removing or covering sensitive items such as food, electronic equipment, and delicate furnishings. It's important to follow the instructions provided by the fogging service provider.

4. **Safety Measures** - Ensure all occupants, including guests and staff, are evacuated from the areas being fogged. Proper signage should be placed to indicate the areas under treatment and to prevent access.

5. **Fogging Process** - The fogging equipment, such as a fogging machine or thermal fogger, is used to disperse the fogging solution as a fine mist into the designated areas. The fog should reach all target surfaces and potential pest harborages or desired sanitization areas.

6. **Exposure Period** - Depending on the fogging product and the intended purpose, there may be a recommended exposure period to allow the fogging solution to take effect. This duration can vary, so it's crucial to follow the instructions provided by the fogging service provider.

7. **Aeration and Ventilation** - After the exposure period, the treated areas should be ventilated to allow for proper air circulation and the dissipation of any

lingering fogging solution or odour. This is typically done by opening windows, using fans, or employing other ventilation methods.

8. **Clean-up and Preparation for Re-entry** - Once the fogging solution has dissipated, the treated areas should be cleaned and prepared for re-entry. This may involve wiping down surfaces, removing any residue, and ensuring that the environment is safe for occupants to return.

9. **Safety Checks and Quality Assurance** - Conduct safety checks and inspections to verify that the fogging process has been completed successfully and that the treated areas are safe for re-entry. It's important to comply with any local regulations and follow the guidelines provided by the fogging service provider.

Remember to work with experienced professionals who are knowledgeable about fogging techniques, the appropriate fogging products for your specific needs, and the safety considerations involved in hotel environments.

Pest issues can be a concern for hotels due to the potential negative impact on guest experience, health and safety, and the hotel's reputation. Here are some common pest issues that hotels may face and the steps taken to address them:

1. **Bed Bugs** - Bed bugs are a significant concern for hotels as they can quickly spread from room to room. Hotels implement proactive measures to prevent bed bug infestations, such as regular inspections of rooms and bedding, staff training on identification and reporting, and the use of mattress encasements. If an infestation is detected, immediate action is taken to treat affected rooms using professional pest control methods.

2. **Cockroaches** - Cockroaches are resilient pests that can thrive in warm and dark areas, such as kitchens, storage rooms, and basements. Hotels maintain strict cleanliness and sanitation practices in these areas to minimize the attraction of cockroaches. Regular inspections, sealing of cracks and crevices, and targeted pest control treatments are performed to prevent and eliminate infestations.

3. **Rodents** - Rats and mice can cause significant damage to a hotel's reputation and infrastructure. Hotels employ preventive measures such as sealing entry points, proper waste management, and regular inspections to prevent rodent access. If rodents are detected, traps or bait stations may be used, and the assistance of professional pest control services may be sought to eliminate the problem.

4. **Ants** - Ants can be a nuisance in hotels, particularly in dining areas and guest rooms. Hotels maintain proper sanitation practices, including prompt clean up of food and beverage spills, to reduce ant attractants. If ant infestations occur, targeted treatments using ant baits or barrier sprays are applied to eliminate the colonies.

5. **Flies and Mosquitoes** - Flies and mosquitoes can disrupt guest comfort, especially in outdoor dining areas and rooms with inadequate screening. Hotels often employ measures such as screens on windows and doors, regular inspection and maintenance of drainage systems, and the use of traps, insecticides, or repellents to control fly and mosquito populations.

6. **Other Pests** - Hotels may encounter other pests, such as fleas, ticks, spiders, or stored product pests. Effective pest management involves identifying the specific pests, implementing appropriate preventive measures, and utilizing targeted treatments or pest control methods tailored to the specific pest species.

To address pest issues effectively, hotels typically work with professional pest management companies. These companies conduct regular inspections, provide guidance on preventive measures, and administer appropriate pest control treatments when necessary. Integrated Pest Management (IPM) techniques are often employed, which involve a combination of proactive measures, monitoring, targeted treatments, and ongoing communication with staff to ensure long-term pest prevention and control.

Overall, hotels prioritize pest management to ensure the comfort, health, and safety of guests, and to protect their reputation. By implementing comprehensive pest control measures and maintaining a clean and sanitary environment, hotels can minimize the risk of pest issues and provide a pleasant experience for their guests.

CHAPTER 15
Façade Cleaning

Facade cleaning is an essential aspect of hotel maintenance to maintain a clean, appealing, and welcoming appearance for guests. The facade of a hotel is the external face of the building, including the walls, windows, and other exterior surfaces. Here are some considerations for facade cleaning in hotels:

1. **Assess the Cleaning Requirements** - Evaluate the condition of the hotel facade and identify the specific cleaning needs. Factors such as the building materials, type and extent of dirt or stains, accessibility, and safety considerations will help determine the appropriate cleaning methods.

2. **Professional Cleaning Services** - Engage a reputable professional cleaning company experienced in facade cleaning for hotels. They will have the expertise, specialized equipment, and knowledge of industry best practices to perform the cleaning efficiently and safely.

3. **Safety Precautions** - Facade cleaning often involves working at heights, so prioritize safety. Ensure that the cleaning company adheres to relevant safety regulations and employs trained personnel who are equipped with proper safety gear, such as harnesses, helmets, and non-slip footwear.

4. **Method Selection** - Various methods can be employed for facade cleaning, depending on the specific requirements. Common techniques include:

- **Pressure Washing** - Suitable for removing dirt, grime, and stains from durable surfaces like concrete, stone, or metal. Care must be taken to adjust the water pressure to prevent damage to delicate surfaces.

- **Chemical Cleaning** - Involves the application of specialized cleaning solutions to dissolve stains or dirt. This method should be performed by professionals who are knowledgeable about the appropriate chemicals and their safe application.

- **Soft Washing** - This technique utilizes low-pressure water combined with biodegradable detergents to clean more delicate surfaces such as painted or rendered walls. Soft washing is ideal for removing organic stains, moss, and mildew.

- **Manual Cleaning** - In cases where the facade has intricate architectural details or fragile elements, manual cleaning using brushes, sponges, or gentle wiping techniques may be necessary.

5. **Window Cleaning** - Window cleaning is a crucial part of facade maintenance. Depending on the height and accessibility of the windows, techniques like water-fed poles, scaffolding, or rope access methods may be employed to ensure a thorough and safe cleaning.

6. **Regular Maintenance** - Establish a regular cleaning and maintenance schedule for the hotel facade to prevent the build up of dirt, stains, or damage. Regular inspections will help identify any issues early on and allow for timely intervention.

7. **Environmental Considerations** - Consider using environmentally friendly cleaning products and methods to minimize the impact on the environment. Discuss this with the cleaning company to ensure their practices align with your sustainability goals.

Remember to consult with professional facade cleaning experts to assess your hotel's specific needs and develop a tailored cleaning plan. By maintaining a clean and attractive facade, you can create a positive first impression for guests and enhance the overall appearance of your hotel

CHAPTER 16
Marble Polishing

Marble polishing is an important aspect of maintaining the aesthetics and longevity of marble surfaces in hotels. Marble is a popular choice for flooring, countertops, and decorative elements in many hotels due to its elegant and luxurious appearance. Here are some considerations for marble polishing in hotels:

1. **Assess the Marble Surfaces** - Evaluate the condition of the marble surfaces throughout the hotel, including floors, walls, reception desks, and other areas. Identify any scratches, stains, or dullness that require polishing.

2. **Professional Marble Polishing Services** - Engage a professional marble polishing company or a specialized stone care service provider. Look for experienced professionals who understand the unique characteristics of marble and have expertise in marble restoration and polishing techniques.

3. **Surface Preparation** - Before polishing, ensure that the marble surfaces are clean and free of any debris, dust, or stains. Thoroughly clean the marble using appropriate stone cleaning products and techniques.

4. **Diamond Polishing Process** - Marble polishing typically involves a process called diamond polishing. This method uses specialized equipment with diamond-encrusted pads to gently grind, smooth, and polish the marble surface.

- **Coarse Grinding** - The first step involves using a coarse-grit diamond pad to remove any scratches, stains, or surface imperfections.

- **Fine Grinding** - Finer-grit diamond pads are then used to further refine the surface and create a smoother finish.

- **Polishing** - Finally, a series of progressively finer-grit diamond pads are used to achieve the desired level of shine and luster on the marble surface.

5. **Honing and Sealing** (if required): In some cases, honing may be necessary to achieve the desired finish. Honing involves using abrasive pads to create a matte or satin finish. Additionally, a stone sealer may be applied to protect the polished marble surface from stains and moisture penetration.

6. **Regular Maintenance** - Develop a regular maintenance plan for the polished marble surfaces to preserve their appearance. This may include regular cleaning using appropriate stone cleaning products, routine inspections for any signs of wear or damage, and prompt addressing of any spills or stains.

7. **Staff Training and Awareness** - Train hotel staff, particularly housekeeping and maintenance teams, on proper marble care and maintenance. Educate them on the importance of using appropriate cleaning products, techniques, and tools to avoid causing damage to the polished marble surfaces.

8. **Preventive Measures** - Implement preventive measures to protect the polished marble surfaces from potential damage. This may include using mats or rugs in high-traffic areas, placing coasters under glasses and other beverages, and promptly cleaning up spills to prevent staining.

Remember that marble is a natural stone, and its care and maintenance require specialized knowledge and techniques. It is advisable to consult with professionals who have experience in marble polishing and maintenance to ensure that the process is performed effectively and in line with the specific requirements of your hotel's marble surfaces.

CHAPTER 17
Carpet Shampooing

Carpet shampooing is an effective method for deep cleaning and maintaining carpets in hotels. Carpets can accumulate dirt, stains, and odors over time, especially in high-traffic areas. Regular carpet shampooing helps to refresh the appearance of the carpets and improve indoor air quality. Here are some considerations for carpet shampooing in hotels:

1. **Professional Carpet Cleaning Services** - Engage a reputable professional carpet cleaning company with experience in commercial settings, including hotels. Look for providers that use appropriate equipment, techniques, and eco-friendly cleaning products.

2. **Pre-Cleaning Inspection** - Conduct a thorough inspection of the carpets to identify any specific areas that require special attention, such as stains, high-traffic zones, or areas with odours. Communicate these details to the carpet cleaning service provider.

3. **Furniture and Room Preparation** - Prior to carpet shampooing, remove any furniture or objects from the carpeted areas. This ensures unobstructed access for the cleaning process. If moving furniture is not feasible, discuss with the cleaning service provider to make appropriate arrangements.

4. **Spot Treatment** - Treat specific stains or spots on the carpet before shampooing. Different types of stains may require different cleaning solutions or techniques. It is important to use suitable products and follow the manufacturer's instructions or seek guidance from the cleaning professionals.

5. **Carpet Shampooing Process** - The carpet cleaning company will use specialized equipment, such as carpet shampooers or extraction machines, for the cleaning process. The steps involved generally include:

- **Pre-vacuuming** - The carpets are vacuumed thoroughly to remove loose dirt and debris.

- **Pre-treatment** - A pre-treatment solution may be applied to the carpets to loosen embedded dirt, stains, and odours.

- **Shampooing** - The carpet shampooer or extraction machine applies a carpet cleaning solution and agitates the carpet fibers to loosen dirt and stains.

- **Extraction** - The machine extracts the dirty solution, along with the suspended dirt and stains, leaving the carpets cleaner.

- **Drying** - Adequate airflow and ventilation should be provided to aid the drying process. It may take a few hours to a day for the carpets to dry completely.

6. **Post-Cleaning Inspection** - After the carpet shampooing process, inspect the carpets to ensure that they have been thoroughly cleaned and any stains or spots have been treated effectively. Address any concerns with the cleaning service provider.

7. **Regular Maintenance** - Develop a regular carpet maintenance schedule, which includes periodic shampooing, vacuuming, and spot cleaning. Regular maintenance helps prolong the life of the carpets and maintains their appearance and cleanliness.

8. **Staff Training** - Train hotel staff, particularly housekeeping teams, on proper carpet care and maintenance practices. Educate them on techniques for spot cleaning, prompt reporting of spills or stains, and the use of appropriate cleaning products and equipment.

Remember, carpets in hotels experience heavy foot traffic, so regular carpet shampooing and maintenance are essential. Working with professional carpet cleaning services and implementing a comprehensive carpet care program will help ensure clean and inviting carpets for hotel guests.

CHAPTER 18
Flower Arrangement

Flower arrangements play a significant role in enhancing the ambiance and aesthetics of hotels. They create a welcoming and visually appealing atmosphere for guests. Here are some considerations for flower arrangement in hotels:

1. **Design Concept** - Determine the overall design concept or theme for the flower arrangements in line with the hotel's style and branding. Consider factors such as the hotel's architecture, interior design, color schemes, and the desired atmosphere (e.g., modern, elegant, tropical, etc.).

2. **Flower Selection** - Choose flowers that complement the design concept and align with the hotel's image. Consider factors such as the season, availability, longevity, fragrance, and colour palette. Opt for flowers that are known for their longevity, such as orchids, lilies, roses, or carnations, to ensure they stay fresh for an extended period.

3. **Vase Selection** - Select vases or containers that enhance the visual appeal of the flower arrangements and complement the hotel's decor. Consider the size, shape, material, and colour of the vases to create a cohesive and balanced look.

4. **Placement** - Determine the strategic placement of flower arrangements within the hotel. Focus on areas such as the lobby, reception desk, dining areas, lounges, or guest rooms. Consider the size of the space, the available surfaces (tables, pedestals, or wall-mounted vases), and the visibility of the arrangements to maximize their impact.

5. **Seasonal and Occasional Themes** - Incorporate seasonal or occasional themes into the flower arrangements. For example, use festive colours and elements during holidays or incorporate seasonal flowers and foliage to reflect the time of year. This adds a touch of freshness and relevance to the hotel's overall decor.

6. **Maintenance and Freshness** - Proper care and maintenance are crucial to ensuring the longevity and freshness of the flower arrangements. Work with experienced floral professionals who can provide advice on watering, pruning, and changing the water regularly. They can also assist with the timely replacement of flowers as needed.

7. **Environmental Considerations** - Consider sustainable and eco-friendly practices when it comes to flower selection and disposal. Opt for locally sourced flowers to support local growers and reduce carbon footprint. Explore options for composting or recycling flower waste.

8. **Budget Management** - Set a budget for flower arrangements and work closely with floral suppliers or professional florists to ensure cost-effective solutions. They can suggest seasonal blooms or alternative flower options that fit within the designated budget without compromising on the overall look and quality.

9. **Safety Considerations** - Ensure that flower arrangements do not obstruct pathways, emergency exits, or pose any safety hazards. Keep in mind allergies and sensitivities of guests or staff members and avoid highly fragrant flowers in areas where they may cause discomfort.

10. **Flexibility and Creativity** - Embrace creativity and adaptability in the flower arrangements. Experiment with different flower combinations, textures, heights, and unique arrangements to create visual interest and surprise guests with refreshing displays.

Remember to periodically assess the flower arrangements and make adjustments as necessary to maintain their freshness, relevance, and visual impact. With careful planning and attention to detail, flower arrangements can contribute to a memorable and inviting experience for hotel guests.

There are various types of flower arrangements that are commonly used in floral design . Here are some of the most popular types:

1. **Bouquet** - A bouquet is a classic flower arrangement consisting of a collection of flowers, often wrapped together with decorative paper or ribbon. It can be hand-held or placed in a vase.

2. **Vase arrangement** - This type of arrangement involves arranging flowers in a vase or container filled with water. It can be a simple arrangement of a single type of flower or a mix of different flowers and foliage.

3. **Floral centrepiece** – Center pieces are larger arrangements designed to be placed in the centre of a table or as a focal point in a room. They can be created using a variety of flowers, foliage, and decorative elements.

4. **Wreath** - A wreath is a circular arrangement typically made from foliage, flowers, or a combination of both. They are commonly used for decorative purposes, particularly during holidays or as memorial tributes.

5. **Corsage** - Corsages are small, wearable flower arrangements often worn on the wrist or pinned to clothing. They are commonly used for special occasions like weddings, proms, or formal events.

6. **Boutonniere** - Similar to corsages, boutonnieres are small floral arrangements designed to be worn by men. They are typically worn on the lapel of a suit or tuxedo for formal events.

7. **Ikebana** - Ikebana is the traditional Japanese art of flower arrangement. It focuses on minimalism, balance, and harmony. Ikebana arrangements often use a small number of carefully chosen flowers and branches placed in specific positions within a container.

8. **Posy** - Posy arrangements are small and compact, typically created by arranging a tight cluster of flowers and tying them together with ribbon or twine. They are often used for gift-giving or as bridal bouquets.

9. **Cascading arrangement** - This type of arrangement features flowers that trail downwards, creating a cascading effect. It is often used in larger, more formal settings, such as weddings or grand events.

10. **Terrarium** - A terrarium arrangement involves placing flowers, foliage, or even small plants inside a glass container, creating a miniature garden. It provides a unique and self-contained display.

These are just a few examples of the many types of flower arrangements available. Floral designers often combine techniques and styles to create unique and personalized arrangements based on the occasion and preferences of their clients.

Flower decoration in hotels is a popular practice that adds beauty, fragrance, and a touch of elegance to various areas within the hotel. Here are some key aspects of flower decoration in hotels:

1. **Lobby and Reception** - Flowers are often used to create stunning floral arrangements in the hotel lobby and reception areas. These arrangements may be placed on reception desks, console tables, or in large vases on pedestals. They create a warm and inviting ambiance for guests as they enter the hotel.

2. **Guest Rooms** - Many hotels incorporate flower arrangements or small floral accents in guest rooms to enhance the overall guest experience. This can be in the form of a vase with fresh flowers on a bedside table, a single flower on a folded towel, or petals scattered on the bed for a romantic touch. The choice of flowers may vary based on the hotel's style, season, and guest preferences.

3. **Restaurants and Dining Areas** - Flowers are often used to adorn dining areas, including tables and buffet stations. Fresh flowers or floral center pieces can add a sophisticated and cheerful touch to the dining experience, creating a visually appealing atmosphere for guests to enjoy their meals.

4. **Event Spaces** - Hotels frequently host weddings, conferences, and other special events. Flower decorations play a vital role in transforming event spaces into beautiful and memorable settings. Large floral arrangements, arches, floral backdrops, and table center pieces are commonly used to enhance the theme and ambiance of the event.

5. **Spa and Wellness Areas** - Flowers can be incorporated into spa and wellness areas to create a tranquil and rejuvenating atmosphere. Small floral accents, such as floating flower petals in baths or on water features, can enhance the sense of relaxation and promote a calming environment.

6. **Outdoor Spaces** - Hotels with outdoor areas often use flowers and plants to enhance the beauty of gardens, courtyards, terraces, and poolside areas. Flowerbeds, hanging baskets, potted plants, and cascading floral arrangements can create a vibrant and picturesque outdoor environment for guests to enjoy.

7. **Special Occasions and Festivals** - Flowers are often used to celebrate special occasions, holidays, or festivals within the hotel. For example, during Valentine's

Day or Christmas, hotels may create elaborate flower displays or themed arrangements to add a festive touch to the overall decor.

8. **Sustainability and Seasonal Choices** - Some hotels prioritize sustainable practices when it comes to flower decoration. They may choose local, seasonal flowers that require less energy-intensive transportation and are in harmony with the natural environment. Using eco-friendly floral foam or incorporating dried flowers and preserved foliage can also be part of sustainable flower decoration practices.

Flower decoration in hotels requires the expertise of skilled florists who understand design principles, colour palettes, and the proper care and handling of flowers. It adds a sense of luxury, elegance, and freshness to various areas of the hotel, enhancing the overall guest experience and creating lasting memories.

CHAPTER 19
Landscaping

Landscaping is an important component of hotel housekeeping that focuses on maintaining and enhancing the outdoor areas of the hotel property. It involves the design, installation, and maintenance of gardens, lawns, plants, trees, and other outdoor features. Here's a closer look at landscaping:

1. **Design and Planning** - The landscaping process begins with designing and planning outdoor spaces to create an aesthetically pleasing and functional environment. This includes selecting suitable plants, trees, and shrubs that complement the hotel's architecture and overall theme. The landscaping design should consider factors like climate, local regulations, guest flow, and maintenance requirements.

2. **Planting and Maintenance** - Landscaping staff is responsible for planting and maintaining the hotel's gardens, flower beds, and green spaces. This involves regular watering, fertilizing, pruning, and pest control to ensure the health and vitality of plants. They also monitor the growth of plants, remove weeds, and replenish mulch or ground cover as needed.

3. **Lawn Care** - Landscaping teams are responsible for maintaining the hotel's lawns by mowing, edging, and trimming grass areas. They also oversee irrigation systems, ensuring that the grass is adequately watered and that irrigation schedules are adjusted based on weather conditions.

4. **Tree and Shrub Care** - Landscapers take care of trees and shrubs on the hotel property, including pruning, shaping, and trimming branches for proper growth and appearance. They may also identify and address any disease or pest issues that could impact the health of the vegetation.

5. **Flower Bed and Planter Maintenance** - Landscaping staff maintains flower beds and planters, ensuring they are well-maintained and visually appealing. This includes planting seasonal flowers, removing spent blooms, and replenishing soil and mulch to maintain a vibrant and colourful display.

6. **Irrigation Systems** - Landscaping teams oversee the operation and maintenance of irrigation systems, ensuring that plants and lawns receive adequate water. They monitor the system for leaks, adjust sprinkler heads, and schedule watering times based on local regulations and weather conditions.

7. **Hardscape Maintenance** - In addition to plants and greenery, landscapers maintain hardscape features such as walkways, patios, fountains, and outdoor seating areas. They ensure these areas are clean, well-maintained, and free from debris or hazards.

8. **Seasonal Landscaping** - Landscaping under hotel housekeeping involves adapting to seasonal changes. This includes planting seasonal flowers and plants, adjusting irrigation schedules, and performing necessary maintenance tasks to ensure the landscape remains attractive and functional throughout the year.

9. **Sustainability Practices** - Landscaping teams may incorporate sustainable practices in their maintenance routines. This can include water conservation techniques, using organic fertilizers, implementing integrated pest management strategies, and selecting native plants that require less water and maintenance.

10. **Collaboration with Other Departments** - Landscaping staff often collaborate with other hotel departments, such as housekeeping, maintenance, and event planning, to ensure that outdoor areas are prepared for special events, weddings, or other functions. They may also coordinate with the engineering department for the maintenance of outdoor lighting and irrigation systems.

Effective landscaping enhances the curb appeal of the hotel, creates a welcoming environment for guests, and contributes to a positive overall guest experience. By maintaining lush gardens, manicured lawns, and attractive outdoor spaces, hotel landscaping teams play a vital role in upholding the hotel's aesthetic standards and providing a relaxing atmosphere for guests to enjoy.

Landscaping plays a significant role in hotels and contributes to the overall guest experience. Here are some key reasons why landscaping is important in hotels:

1. **Aesthetics and Curb Appeal** - Landscaping enhances the visual appeal of the hotel's exterior, creating a welcoming and attractive first impression for guests. Well-designed gardens, manicured lawns, colourful flower beds, and thoughtfully placed trees and shrubs contribute to a visually pleasing environment.

2. **Relaxing and Serene Atmosphere** - Hotels often strive to provide a peaceful and tranquil ambiance for guests. Beautifully landscaped outdoor areas offer a serene retreat where guests can relax, unwind, and enjoy nature. The presence of greenery and natural elements creates a calming atmosphere that can help guests de-stress and rejuvenate.

3. **Enhanced Guest Experience** - The overall guest experience is greatly influenced by the hotel's surroundings. Well-maintained landscapes provide pleasant areas for guests to stroll, sit, or enjoy outdoor activities. It offers opportunities for guests to connect with nature, take memorable photographs, or simply enjoy the scenery.

4. **Outdoor Event Spaces** - Hotels often host events such as weddings, parties, and corporate gatherings. Landscaped outdoor areas provide attractive venues for these events. Beautiful gardens, courtyards, and outdoor patios offer a picturesque backdrop, creating a memorable setting for special occasions.

5. **Brand Image and Differentiation** - Landscaping can contribute to a hotel's brand image and differentiate it from competitors. Unique and well-maintained landscapes that reflect the hotel's theme or location can become defining features that set the hotel apart and make it more memorable to guests.

6. **Environmental Sustainability** - Landscaping can incorporate sustainable practices that align with the hotel's environmental initiatives. This may include using native plants that require less water and maintenance, implementing water-efficient irrigation systems, and employing organic fertilizers or pest control methods. These practices demonstrate the hotel's commitment to sustainability and can be appreciated by environmentally conscious guests.

7. **Outdoor Dining and Recreation** - Hotels often have outdoor dining areas, patios, or recreational facilities. Landscaping enhances these spaces, providing a pleasant outdoor environment for guests to enjoy their meals or engage in

recreational activities. Well-designed landscapes create an inviting atmosphere and contribute to the overall dining or leisure experience.

8. **Improved Property Value** - A well-maintained and landscaped exterior can enhance the overall value of the hotel property. Landscaping adds to the aesthetic appeal and desirability of the hotel, potentially attracting more guests and positively influencing the property's market value.

In summary, landscaping in hotels is important for creating an attractive, relaxing, and memorable guest experience. It contributes to the hotel's curb appeal, brand image, and overall ambiance. Additionally, well-designed landscapes provide opportunities for outdoor activities, events, and sustainable practices, all of which can enhance the hotel's reputation and value

CHAPTER 20
Chandelier Cleaning

Chandelier cleaning is an important task to maintain the beauty and functionality of these decorative lighting fixtures. Chandeliers are often the focal point of a room and can accumulate dust, dirt, and grime over time. Here are some considerations for chandelier cleaning:

Chandelier cleaning in hotels requires special attention due to the size, height, and complexity of the fixtures. Here are some considerations for chandelier cleaning in hotels:

1. **Safety Precautions** - Prioritize safety during the chandelier cleaning process. Make sure to follow all relevant safety guidelines and regulations. Use appropriate personal protective equipment (PPE) such as gloves, safety glasses, and even a harness if necessary. Consider working with a professional chandelier cleaning service that has experience in hotel settings.

2. **Evaluation and Planning** - Assess the chandelier's condition and complexity to determine the appropriate cleaning method. Take note of any fragile components, intricate details, or delicate materials that may require special care. Plan the cleaning process, considering access to the chandelier, available equipment, and any necessary protective measures for surrounding furniture or surfaces.

3. **Professional Chandelier Cleaning Services** - Engage a professional chandelier cleaning company experienced in handling large-scale chandelier cleaning projects. They will have the expertise, equipment, and knowledge of safety protocols to clean chandeliers effectively and efficiently.

4. **Cleaning Methods:**

- **Dry Dusting** - Start by using a soft, dry cloth or a feather duster to remove loose dust and debris from the chandelier. Be cautious and avoid applying pressure that could damage delicate parts.

- **Wet Cleaning** - Depending on the chandelier's material and condition, a wet cleaning method may be appropriate. This can involve using a mild cleaning solution or a mixture of water and gentle soap. Apply the solution sparingly to a soft cloth or sponge and gently wipe the chandelier's surface. Avoid excessive moisture and be cautious around electrical components.

- **Professional Cleaning Techniques** - Professional chandelier cleaning services may utilize specialized tools and techniques such as ultrasonic cleaning or steam cleaning for more intricate or delicate chandeliers. These methods can effectively remove stubborn grime and restore the chandelier's shine.

5. **Regular Maintenance** - Establish a regular chandelier maintenance schedule to prevent excessive dirt build-up. Regular dusting and cleaning can help prolong the intervals between more extensive cleaning sessions.

6. **Access and Height Considerations** - Chandeliers in hotels are often positioned at considerable heights, making access a challenge. Ensure proper access equipment, such as ladders or scaffolding, is used safely and in compliance with safety regulations. If necessary, consult professional cleaning services experienced in working at heights.

7. **Documentation and Quality Control** - Keep records of chandelier cleaning dates and details, including any specific instructions or recommendations provided by the cleaning service. Regularly inspect the chandeliers after cleaning to ensure they meet the desired cleanliness standards.

8. **Staff Training** - Train hotel staff, particularly maintenance and housekeeping teams, on chandelier cleaning protocols and safety measures. Familiarize them with the specific requirements and techniques for handling and cleaning different types of chandeliers.

Remember that chandelier cleaning in hotels requires careful planning, specialized equipment, and expertise. Working with professionals who understand the intricacies of chandelier cleaning will help ensure the chandeliers in your hotel are maintained in pristine condition and continue to enhance the overall aesthetic appeal of your establishment.

CHAPTER 21
Snagging

Snagging refers to the process of identifying and rectifying any defects or issues in a newly constructed or renovated hotel before its final handover or opening. It involves a detailed inspection to identify and document any incomplete or faulty work, construction defects, or areas that do not meet the agreed-upon specifications or quality standards. Here are some considerations for snagging in hotels:

1. **Snagging Inspection** - Conduct a thorough inspection of the entire hotel, including guest rooms, public areas, back-of-house spaces, and exterior areas. Pay close attention to finishes, fixtures, fittings, utilities, and any other relevant aspects. Use a checklist to systematically document any snags or issues.

2. **Defect Identification** - Identify and document any defects, deficiencies, or non-compliant items. This may include issues such as uneven flooring, damaged walls, malfunctioning fixtures, poor paintwork, electrical or plumbing problems, or incomplete installations. Take note of both visual defects and functional issues.

3. **Categorize Snags** - Categorize the identified snags based on their severity and urgency for rectification. Prioritize critical snags that impact safety, functionality, or guest experience. This allows the responsible parties to address the most significant issues promptly.

4. **Communication and Documentation** - Create a comprehensive snagging report that includes detailed descriptions, photographs, and locations of each snag. Assign responsibility for each item to the relevant contractor, subcontractor, or project team member. Share the snagging report with the responsible parties and maintain open lines of communication throughout the rectification process.

5. **Rectification Process** - Coordinate with the responsible parties to ensure that each snag is addressed and resolved promptly. Monitor the progress of snag rectification, track completion, and request appropriate documentation or evidence of corrective actions taken. Conduct follow-up inspections to verify that the identified snags have been effectively resolved.

6. **Snag Management Software** - Consider utilizing snag management software or digital tools to streamline the snagging process. These tools can facilitate the documentation, tracking, and communication of snags, making the entire process more efficient and organized.

7. **Final Inspection** - Conduct a final inspection after the snag rectification process to ensure that all snags have been resolved to the required standards. Verify that the quality of workmanship, finishes, and installations meet the agreed-upon specifications and expectations.

8. **Ongoing Maintenance** - Implement a proactive maintenance plan to address any recurring or emerging issues beyond the snagging process. Regularly inspect and maintain the hotel's facilities and systems to ensure their continued functionality and optimal performance.

Snagging is a crucial step in ensuring that a newly constructed or renovated hotel meets the expected quality standards and provides a positive guest experience. Thorough snagging, effective communication, and diligent rectification efforts contribute to a successful project handover and set the stage for the hotel's long-term operational success.

CHAPTER 22
Lost & Found Management

Lost & Found services are an essential part of hotel operations, providing a way to reunite guests with their lost belongings. Here are some considerations for managing Lost & Found in hotels:

1. **Designated Lost & Found Area** - Set up a dedicated Lost & Found area within the hotel where found items can be securely stored. This area should be easily accessible to both guests and staff members. Implement a system for organizing and tracking lost items to ensure efficient retrieval.

2. **Clear Procedures and Policies** - Establish clear procedures and policies for handling lost items. Train the hotel staff, especially front desk personnel and housekeeping staff, on these procedures to ensure consistency in handling and documenting lost items. Define the timeframe for holding lost items before disposal or donation, and determine the process for returning items to their rightful owners.

3. **Guest Communication** - Inform guests about the Lost & Found services during check-in or through informational materials in guest rooms. Provide guests with clear instructions on how to report lost items and how to retrieve them. Offer multiple channels of communication, such as phone, email, or an online Lost & Found form, to accommodate different guest preferences.

4. **Prompt Reporting and Documentation** - Train staff members to promptly report and document any found items. Maintain a detailed record of each lost item, including a description, date found, location found, and any relevant guest information (room number, contact details, etc.). Use a digital system or a logbook to track the details of found items and their disposition.

5. **Item Storage and Security** - Ensure that the Lost & Found area is secure and accessible only to authorized personnel. Implement measures to prevent theft or loss of items in storage. Consider using lockable storage cabinets or rooms, surveillance cameras, or restricted access protocols to protect lost items.

6. **Guest Verification** - Establish procedures for verifying ownership of lost items before releasing them to guests. Require guests to provide appropriate identification or proof of ownership, such as a matching description or photo of the lost item, to ensure that items are returned to the rightful owners.

7. **Communication with Guests** - Maintain regular communication with guests regarding their lost items. Provide updates on the status of the search or retrieval process and inform guests of any relevant charges or procedures for shipping or returning items. Keep a record of all interactions with guests regarding lost items for reference.

8. **Disposal or Donation** - Establish a policy for disposing of unclaimed items or donating them to charitable organizations after a specified period of time. Ensure compliance with local laws and regulations regarding the disposal of lost items.

9. **Continuous Improvement** - Regularly review and assess Lost & Found procedures to identify areas for improvement. Seek guest feedback to gauge their satisfaction with the Lost & Found services and implement any necessary adjustments based on guest input.

Efficient Lost & Found management demonstrates a hotel's commitment to guest satisfaction and customer service. By implementing clear procedures, maintaining effective communication, and ensuring the security of lost items, hotels can provide a reliable and helpful Lost & Found service for their guests.

CHAPTER 23
Standard Operating Procedures

Standard Operating Procedures (SOPs) in hotels are essential guidelines and protocols that establish consistent and efficient practices for various hotel operations. SOPs help ensure that hotel staff members understand their roles and responsibilities, maintain quality standards, and provide a seamless experience for guests. While specific SOPs may vary based on the hotel's size, type, and brand, here are some common areas where SOPs are implemented :

1. **Front Desk Operations:**

- Check-in and check-out procedures
- Guest registration and identification verification
- Handling guest inquiries and complaints
- Room allocation and assignment
- Cash handling and payment processes
- Key control and security protocols

2. **Housekeeping:**

- Cleaning and sanitization procedures for guest rooms, public areas, and back-of-house areas
- Bed-making and linen/towel changing protocols
- Restocking amenities and supplies in guest rooms
- Lost & Found procedures
- Maintenance reporting for room repairs or equipment issues

- Handling guest privacy and security

3. **Food and Beverage:**

- Food preparation, handling, and storage guidelines
- Service standards for breakfast, lunch, dinner, and room service
- Table setting and arrangement
- Order taking and processing
- Bar service and responsible alcohol service
- Billing and cash handling procedures

4. **Concierge Services:**

- Assistance with guest requests, such as transportation, reservations, or local recommendations
- Luggage handling and storage procedures
- Handling special requests or VIP services
- Coordination of guest arrivals and departures
- Providing information on hotel amenities and facilities

5. **Security and Safety:**

- Emergency response procedures (fire, medical emergencies, etc.)
- Surveillance and access control protocols
- Reporting and handling security incidents
- Lost and stolen item procedures
- Safety training and awareness for staff members
- Implementing health and safety measures, such as COVID-19 protocols

6. **Sales and Marketing:**

- Sales techniques and procedures for room reservations and group bookings

- Upselling and cross-selling strategies
- Handling guest feedback and reviews
- Loyalty program enrollment and benefits explanation
- Promotional offers and packages implementation

7. **Human Resources:**

- Recruitment and onboarding processes
- Staff training and development programs
- Employee scheduling and attendance management
- Performance evaluation and disciplinary procedures
- Employee benefits and policies
- Health and safety guidelines for staff members

These are just a few examples of the many areas where SOPs are implemented in hotels. SOPs ensure that hotel operations are streamlined, consistent, and aligned with the hotel's brand and quality standards . They serve as valuable resources for training new employees, maintaining consistency across departments, and delivering a high level of service to guests.

Standard Operating Procedures (SOPs) for hotel housekeeping are essential guidelines that ensure consistency, efficiency, and quality in the cleaning and maintenance of hotel rooms and public areas. Here are some common SOPs followed by hotel housekeeping departments:

1. **Room Cleaning:**

a. **Preparing the cart** - Gather all necessary cleaning supplies, linens, amenities, and equipment before starting room cleaning.

b. **Knock and announce** - Knock on the guest's door and announce "Housekeeping" before entering.

c. **Dusting and vacuuming** - Dust all surfaces, including furniture, fixtures, and electronics. Vacuum carpets, rugs, and upholstery.

d. **Bed making** - Strip and replace used bed linens, tuck and fold sheets, fluff pillows, and arrange blankets or duvets.

e. **Bathroom cleaning** - Clean and sanitize the bathroom, including the toilet, sink, bathtub or shower, mirrors, and countertops. Replenish toiletries and towels.

f. **Floor cleaning** - Sweep and mop the floors, paying attention to corners and hard-to-reach areas.

g. **Trash removal** - Empty waste bins and replace trash bags.

h. **Final touches** - Arrange furniture, adjust curtains or blinds, and ensure the room is neat and presentable.

2. **Public Area Cleaning:**

a. **Reception and lobby** - Clean and polish the reception desk, furniture, and fixtures. Vacuum or sweep and mop the floors. Wipe glass surfaces and remove any litter.

b. **Hallways and corridors** - Vacuum or sweep and mop the floors. Dust and wipe handrails, doors, and signage. Remove any obstructions or hazards.

c. **Elevators** - Clean and polish elevator doors, buttons, and interior surfaces. Ensure proper functioning and report any issues to maintenance.

d. **Restrooms** - Clean and sanitize toilets, sinks, mirrors, countertops, and floors. Replenish toiletries and towels. Empty and sanitize trash bins.

e. **Fitness center and pool area** - Clean and sanitize exercise equipment, surfaces, and poolside furniture. Ensure towels are stocked and the area is well-maintained .

f. **Stairwells** - Sweep or vacuum the stairs, clean handrails, and ensure proper lighting and safety.

3. **Linen and Laundry Management:**

a. **Sorting and inventory** - Sort linens based on type and condition. Maintain an accurate inventory to ensure an adequate supply of clean linens.

b. **Washing and drying** - Follow proper laundering procedures, including using appropriate detergents and temperatures. Dry linens thoroughly.

c. **Folding and storage** - Fold and stack linens neatly and store them in designated areas, keeping them organized and easily accessible.

4. <u>**Reporting and Communication**</u>:

a. **Maintenance issues** - Report any maintenance issues or equipment malfunctions promptly.

b. **Lost and found** - Follow the hotel's lost and found procedures to properly handle and document any lost items.

c. **Communication with colleagues** - Maintain effective communication with other housekeeping staff, supervisors, and front desk personnel to ensure smooth operations and guest satisfaction.

Remember, SOPs may vary between hotels, and it's important to adapt them to the specific needs and requirements of your establishment. Regular training and supervision of housekeeping staff are crucial to ensure SOPs are followed consistently and updated as necessary .

CHAPTER 24

Do Not Disturb Procedure

DND, which stands for "Do Not Disturb," is a common request from hotel guests who prefer not to have their rooms cleaned or disturbed during their stay. It is important for hotels to have clear procedures in place to respect guests' privacy while also ensuring the safety and satisfaction of all guests. Here's an outline of the typical DND procedure in hotels:

1. **Guest Communication** - During check-in or upon arrival, inform guests about the DND policy and procedure. Clearly explain the purpose and benefits of the DND option, such as maintaining privacy, uninterrupted rest, or working without disturbances. Provide information on how to request the DND service.

2. **DND Signage** - Provide a DND sign or door hanger for guests to indicate their preference. This can be a simple "Do Not Disturb" sign or a hanger that can be hung on the outside doorknob of the guest room.

3. **Guest Room Check-In** - Instruct front desk staff to inform guests during check-in about the location and usage of the DND sign. Explain that placing the sign on the outside doorknob indicates the guest's desire for privacy and that housekeeping staff will not enter the room for cleaning or maintenance purposes.

4. **Housekeeping Awareness** - Train housekeeping staff to look for the DND sign or indicator before entering guest rooms. Emphasize the importance of respecting guest privacy and following the DND policy. Instruct staff to adhere to the established procedures and not to enter a room with a DND sign unless there is an emergency or a specific request from the guest.

5. **DND Duration** - Clarify the duration of the DND status. Some hotels may allow guests to keep the DND sign for the entire duration of their stay, while others

may require guests to remove the sign daily for regular housekeeping or maintenance.

6. **Alternate Services** - Provide alternative options for guests who choose the DND service. This may include offering scheduled housekeeping services at specific times when the guest is not in the room or providing additional amenities and supplies upon request.

7. **Guest Request fulfillment** - Encourage guests to communicate their needs or requests to the front desk if they have the DND sign on their door. Ensure that staff members are responsive and attentive to these requests, such as providing extra towels, toiletries, or room service items.

8. **Communication with Housekeeping** - Establish a process for communication between the front desk and housekeeping regarding rooms with DND signs. This ensures that staff members are aware of the DND status and can adjust their cleaning schedules accordingly.

9. **DND Sign Removal** - Remind guests to remove the DND sign when they no longer require privacy or when they are checking out. Inform guests that housekeeping staff will resume regular cleaning and maintenance services once the DND sign is removed.

10. **Monitoring and Quality Control** - Implement regular checks and monitoring procedures to ensure compliance with the DND policy. Supervisors or managers should periodically review housekeeping records and address any issues or concerns related to DND requests.

It is important to strike a balance between respecting guest privacy and maintaining the cleanliness and safety standards of the hotel. By establishing a clear DND procedure and effectively communicating it to guests and staff members, hotels can ensure that guests' privacy preferences are honored while still providing a pleasant and comfortable stay experience

CHAPTER 25
Lobby Scenting

Scenting in hotels, also known as ambient scenting or fragrance branding, is a practice where a particular scent or fragrance is introduced into the hotel environment to enhance the guest experience. Here are some considerations for scenting in hotels:

1. **Purpose and Branding** - Determine the purpose and objectives of scenting in relation to your hotel's brand identity. The chosen scent should align with the hotel's image, create a welcoming atmosphere, and enhance the overall guest experience.

2. **Scent Selection** - Choose a scent that is pleasant, subtle, and appropriate for the hotel environment. Consider factors such as the hotel's location, target market, and the ambiance you want to create. Common scent categories include floral, citrus, woody, or fresh scents, but it is important to test and select a scent that resonates with your brand.

3. **Professional Scenting Services** - Engage a professional scenting company or consultant that specializes in ambient scenting. They can help you select the right scent, install scenting equipment, and provide ongoing maintenance and support.

4. **Scenting Areas** - Determine the areas of the hotel where scenting will be implemented. This may include the lobby, reception area, corridors, guest rooms, spa, fitness center, or other public spaces. Consider the size and layout of each area when determining the appropriate scenting equipment and intensity.

5. **Scent Diffusion Systems** - Install scent diffusion systems that can effectively disperse the chosen scent throughout the designated areas. These systems may use various technologies such as HVAC scenting, cold-air diffusion, or

standalone scent diffusers. Consult with scenting professionals to determine the most suitable system for your hotel.

6. **Scenting Intensity and Timing** - Adjust the intensity and timing of scent diffusion to create the desired effect. For example, you may want a stronger scent in the lobby during peak hours and a lighter scent in guest rooms during turndown service. Test different settings to achieve the right balance.

7. **Guest Sensitivities and Preferences** - Be mindful of guests with sensitivities or allergies to certain scents. Consider offering scent-free areas or providing alternative options for guests who prefer not to be exposed to scents. Communicate with guests about the scenting program, and be responsive to their feedback or concerns.

8. **Consistency and Maintenance** - Ensure consistent scenting across different areas of the hotel. Regularly monitor and maintain scenting equipment to ensure proper functioning and prevent any unpleasant odours or disruptions.

9. **Brand Extension** - Consider extending the scenting experience beyond the hotel environment. Develop scented amenities such as soaps, shampoos, or candles that carry the signature scent, allowing guests to take the experience home with them.

10. **Evaluation and Feedback** - Continuously evaluate the impact of scenting on guest experience and satisfaction. Collect guest feedback and monitor online reviews to gauge the effectiveness of the chosen scent and adjust the scenting program as needed.

Scenting can contribute to a memorable and immersive guest experience, creating a positive and lasting impression. By carefully selecting scents that align with the hotel's brand and implementing scenting strategies in a thoughtful and guest-centric manner, hotels can enhance the overall ambiance and elevate the sensory experience for their guests

CHAPTER 26
Latest Trends & Technologies

The housekeeping industry is constantly evolving, with new trends and technologies emerging to improve efficiency, sustainability, and guest satisfaction. Here are some of the latest trends and technologies in housekeeping:

1. **Automation and Robotics** - The use of automation and robotics is increasing in housekeeping operations. Robotic vacuum cleaners, automated linen sorting systems, and robotic window cleaners are being employed to streamline tasks and reduce manual labour.

2. **IOT (Internet of Things) and Smart Housekeeping** - IOT technology allows for connectivity between devices and systems. In housekeeping, IOT-enabled devices such as smart thermostats, energy management systems, and smart locks are used to enhance energy efficiency, automate room controls, and monitor housekeeping activities.

3. **Mobile Applications and Digital Tools** - Housekeeping staff are using mobile applications and digital tools for task management, room assignments, inventory tracking, and communication. These tools streamline operations, provide real-time updates, and facilitate efficient collaboration among team members.

4. **Green Cleaning Practices** - Sustainability and eco-friendliness are key considerations in housekeeping. Green cleaning practices involve using environmentally friendly cleaning products, minimizing water and energy consumption, and implementing waste management strategies to reduce the ecological footprint.

5. **UV-C Disinfection** - Ultraviolet-C (UV-C) disinfection technology is gaining popularity for its effectiveness in killing bacteria and viruses. UV-C devices are

used for disinfecting high-touch surfaces, including bedding, upholstery, and bathroom fixtures, to enhance cleanliness and guest safety.

6. **Electrostatic Sprayers** - Electrostatic sprayers are used for efficient and thorough disinfection. These devices electrically charge disinfectant particles, enabling them to adhere to surfaces evenly, including hard-to-reach areas. Electrostatic sprayers can help improve cleanliness and sanitation protocols.

7. **Virtual Reality (VR) Training** - VR training programs are being adopted in housekeeping to enhance staff training and on-boarding processes. Virtual reality simulations provide a realistic environment for learning and practicing housekeeping tasks, improving efficiency and reducing errors.

8. **Data Analytics and Performance Monitoring** - Housekeeping operations are leveraging data analytics tools to monitor performance, identify trends, and optimize resource allocation. Key metrics such as room turnaround time, housekeeping productivity, and guest satisfaction scores are analyzed to improve operational efficiency.

9. **RFID (Radio Frequency Identification)** - RFID technology is used for inventory management and tracking of linens, uniforms, and supplies. RFID tags and readers enable real-time tracking, reduce losses, and improve inventory accuracy in housekeeping operations.

10. **Sustainable Linen and Towel Programs** - Many hotels are implementing sustainable linen and towel programs to conserve water and energy. Guests are encouraged to reuse towels and linens during their stay, reducing unnecessary laundering and promoting environmental responsibility.

It's important for housekeeping departments to stay updated on these trends and technologies, carefully considering their suitability and benefits for their specific hotel's operations. Implementing the right innovations can improve efficiency, reduce costs, enhance sustainability practices, and contribute to an excellent guest experience.

CHAPTER 27
Audits

Housekeeping audits in hotels are essential to assess the cleanliness, efficiency, and overall quality of housekeeping operations. These audits help ensure that established standards and procedures are followed, identify areas for improvement, and maintain a high level of guest satisfaction. Here are some key aspects of housekeeping audits in hotels:

1. **Audit Frequency** - Establish a regular schedule for conducting housekeeping audits. The frequency may vary depending on factors such as hotel size, occupancy levels, and brand standards. Audits can be conducted daily, weekly, monthly, or quarterly.

2. **Audit Checklist** - Develop a comprehensive checklist that covers all aspects of housekeeping operations. The checklist should include items related to room cleanliness, bed and linen quality, bathroom condition, public area maintenance, inventory control, and adherence to standard operating procedures (SOPs).

3. **Quality Standards** - Clearly define the quality standards that housekeeping staff should meet. This includes expectations for cleanliness, orderliness, attention to detail, and adherence to brand-specific requirements. Standards may also encompass factors such as odour control, proper maintenance of equipment, and safety protocols.

4. **Audit Process** - Determine the process for conducting housekeeping audits. This may involve a combination of scheduled audits and surprise inspections. Designate trained auditors who will evaluate the designated areas and complete the audit checklist objectively.

5. **Documentation** - Maintain thorough documentation of the audit process. This includes recording the date, time, and location of the audit, as well as the

auditor's name. Document any findings, observations, and recommendations for improvement. Use a standardized format or digital system for consistency and easy reference.

6. **Corrective Actions** - When deficiencies or areas for improvement are identified during audits, establish a system for documenting and addressing these issues. Assign responsibilities for implementing corrective actions and establish a timeline for completion. Regularly monitor progress and verify that corrective measures have been effectively implemented .

7. **Training and Development** - Use audit findings as opportunities for training and development. Identify recurring issues or knowledge gaps and provide additional training or reinforcement to housekeeping staff. This can include refresher courses on cleaning techniques, proper product usage, and best practices for maintaining quality standards.

8. **Continuous Improvement** - Treat housekeeping audits as a continuous improvement process. Regularly review audit results, identify trends, and make adjustments to procedures or training programs as needed. Solicit feedback from guests regarding their housekeeping experience and integrate that feedback into the audit process.

9. **Recognition and Incentives** - Recognize and reward high-performing housekeeping teams based on audit results. Establish incentives or recognition programs that motivate staff to maintain and exceed quality standards. This can help foster a culture of excellence and enhance morale.

10. **Follow-Up Audits** - Conduct follow-up audits to verify the effectiveness of corrective actions and ensure sustained improvement. These audits help monitor progress, identify any new issues, and ensure ongoing adherence to established standards.

Housekeeping audits play a crucial role in maintaining cleanliness, efficiency, and guest satisfaction in hotels. By conducting regular audits, addressing areas for improvement, and continuously monitoring performance, hotels can consistently deliver exceptional housekeeping services.

The housekeeping budget process involves planning, allocating, and managing financial resources for the housekeeping department of a hotel or hospitality establishment. Here are the key steps involved in the housekeeping budget process:

1. **Forecasting** - Begin by forecasting the anticipated housekeeping needs for the upcoming budget period. Consider factors such as projected occupancy rates, room turnover, guest expectations, and any planned changes or renovations that may affect the workload or requirements of the department.

2. **Expense Analysis** - Review historical data and analyze the expenses incurred by the housekeeping department in the previous budget period. Identify major expense categories, such as labour costs, cleaning supplies, laundry services, equipment maintenance, and uniforms. Assess any cost variances and identify areas for potential cost savings or efficiency improvements.

3. **Revenue Projections** - Collaborate with the revenue management team to obtain revenue projections for the hotel. This information helps estimate the financial resources available for the housekeeping department. Revenue projections can be based on occupancy rates, room rates, and other revenue-generating areas such as meeting spaces or additional services offered by the hotel.

4. **Budget Allocation** - Based on the forecasting, expense analysis, and revenue projections, allocate financial resources to different expense categories within the housekeeping department. Consider factors such as labour costs, cleaning supplies, laundry services, equipment upgrades or replacements, training and development, and any other specific needs of the department.

5. **Cost Control Measures** - Implement cost control measures to ensure that expenses are managed within the allocated budget. This may involve monitoring and tracking expenses regularly, negotiating contracts with suppliers to obtain competitive pricing, optimizing staffing levels and schedules, implementing energy-saving initiatives, and seeking opportunities for process improvements and cost efficiencies.

6. **Budget Approval** - Present the proposed housekeeping budget to the relevant stakeholders, such as the hotel general manager, financial controller, or executive team, for review and approval. Address any questions or concerns raised during the review process and make adjustments as necessary.

7. **Monitoring and Reporting** - Once the budget is approved, closely monitor expenses and compare them to the budgeted amounts on an ongoing basis. Regularly generate financial reports to track actual expenses, identify any deviations from the budget, and provide updates to the management team. This allows for timely adjustments and corrective actions if needed.

8. **Budget Revisions** - Throughout the budget period, reassess the budget periodically to reflect any changes in business conditions, guest demands, or unforeseen circumstances. Adjust the budget as necessary to ensure it remains realistic and aligned with the current needs and priorities of the housekeeping department.

By following these steps, the housekeeping department can effectively plan and manage its financial resources, ensuring that it can meet the operational needs while controlling costs and maximizing efficiency.

Write to me at behl.pankaj2012@gmail.com

Or DM on Insta to connect further

www.ingramcontent.com/pod-product-compliance
Lightning Source LLC
LaVergne TN
LVHW070526070526
838199LV00073B/6714